SAUCES

SAUCES

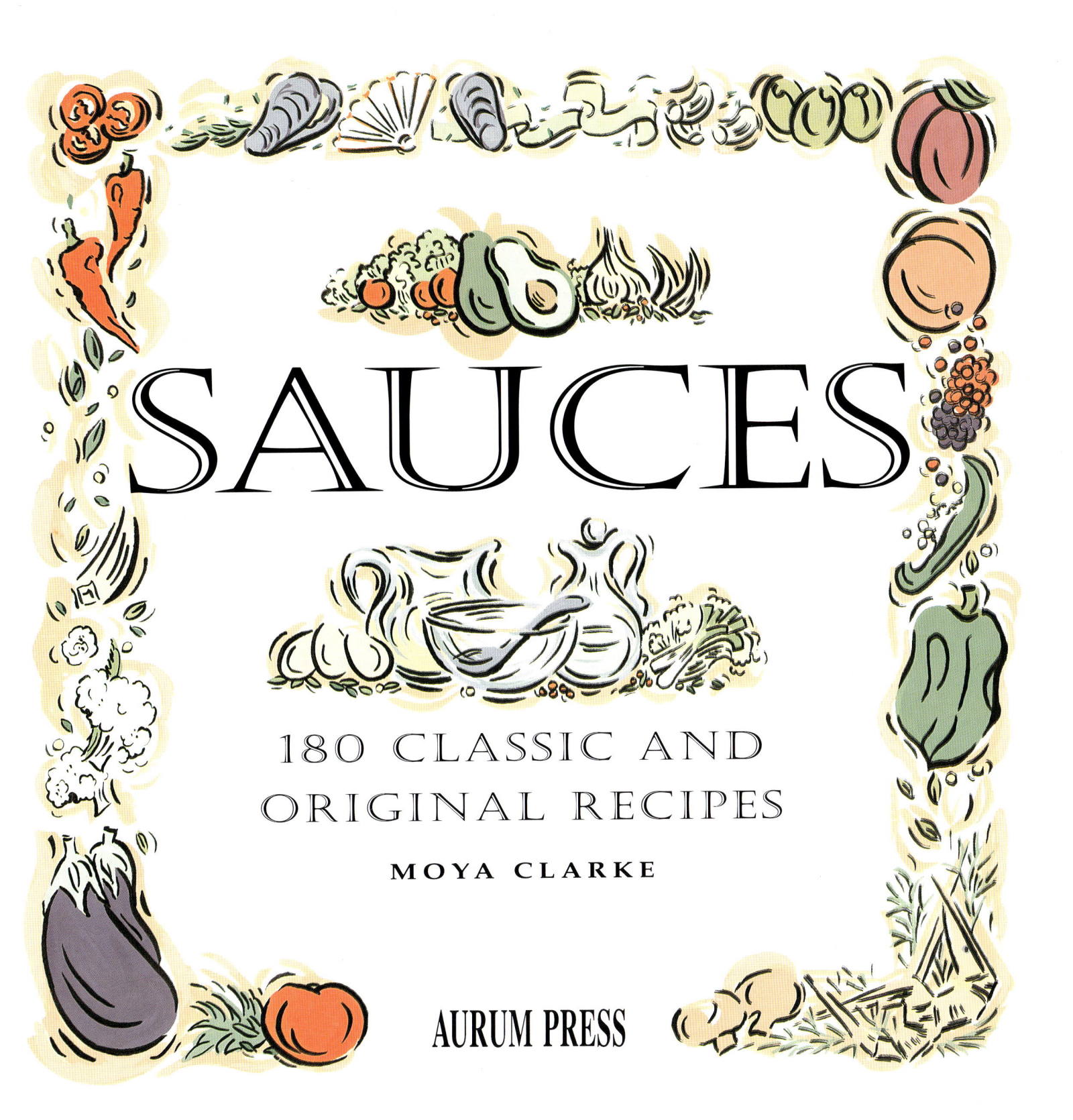

180 CLASSIC AND ORIGINAL RECIPES

MOYA CLARKE

AURUM PRESS

A QUINTET BOOK

First published 1994 by
Aurum Press Ltd
25 Bedford Avenue
London WC1B 3AT

Copyright © 1994 Quintet Publishing
Limited. All rights reserved. No part of this
publication may be reproduced, stored in a
retrieval system or transmitted in any form
or by any means, electronic, mechanical,
photocopying, recording or otherwise,
without the permission of the copyright
holder.

A catalogue record for this book is available
from the British Library

ISBN 1-85410-305-9

2 4 6 8 10 9 7 5 3 1
1995 1997 1998 1996 1994

This book was designed and produced by
Quintet Publishing Limited
6 Blundell Street
London N7 9BH

Creative Director: Richard Dewing
Designer: Ian Hunt
Project Editor: Anna Briffa
Illustrator: Joanne Makin

Typeset in Great Britain by
Central Southern Typesetters, Eastbourne
Manufactured in Singapore by Bright Arts Pte. Ltd.
Printed in Singapore by Star Standard Industries Pte. Ltd.

Contents

CHAPTER ONE   Discovering Sauces **6**

CHAPTER TWO   From Saucepan to Sauceboat **13**

CHAPTER THREE   Foundation Sauces **16**

CHAPTER FOUR   Classic Sauces **23**

CHAPTER FIVE   Vegetable Sauces **34**

CHAPTER SIX   Pasta Sauces **42**

CHAPTER SEVEN   Sauces from Around the World **46**

CHAPTER EIGHT   Savoury Fruit Sauces **51**

CHAPTER NINE   Cold Sauces and Relishes **56**

CHAPTER TEN   Marinades and Dressings **61**

CHAPTER ELEVEN   Creams, Custards and Milk Sauces **66**

CHAPTER TWELVE   The Sweeter Sauces **71**

CHAPTER THIRTEEN   What Goes With What **77**

Index **80**

CHAPTER ONE

Discovering Sauces

~

Every sauce plays a vital role in the dish in which it features and its part in the menu is equally important. A sauce should do more than add moisture: it should enhance a dish by heightening its flavour, contribute to the colour of the meal, and possibly add texture as well.

A sauce is a carefully flavoured, well-balanced liquid. Some are thickened, while others are thin but are reduced to concentrate the flavour. The majority of classic sauces rely on basic recipes, usually referred to as foundation sauces. These are well worth mastering, as they direct the cook towards a wide range of variations.

If you are inexperienced at making sauces, start by making everyday recipes and simple dressings – a white sauce, for example, or a French dressing. Then you can experiment with these before extending your repertoire to include more adventurous liaisons.

CLASSIFICATION OF SAUCES

A sauce can be extremely simple, such as melted butter sharpened with lemon juice and flavoured with herbs, or a sweet, warmed syrup. More complex sauces involve the use of thickening agents, such as fat, flour or egg yolks. The liquid used to make a sauce can vary from stock or milk to wine, with the addition of cream or other enriching liquids.

One method of categorizing the different sauces is to divide them according to the thickening used:

Unthickened Sauces

These include sauces based on melted butter, reduced liquids, and dressings, such as mint sauce or vinaigrette. Unthickened sweet sauces include syrups and simple flavoured yogurt or cream mixtures.

Roux-based Sauces

A roux is a mixture of fat and flour cooked together to form a paste. It may be cooked for just a few minutes (for a blond roux to thicken pale sauces) or for longer to brown the flour (for a brown sauce or gravy). Then the liquid is gradually added and the mixture is stirred vigorously the whole time to prevent lumps forming. There are several schools of thought about whether the liquid should be added on high or low heat, off the heat or how quickly. The most successful method is to add the liquid over medium heat and to judge the speed at which it thickens. If the liquid is poured in too fast, the benefit of the roux is lost to some extent and the sauce won't thicken, whereas if you add the liquid a little at a time, it heats up rapidly and the sauce thickens quickly so there is less danger of lumps forming. If the mixture begins to thicken too quickly, however, then the stirring has to be quite vigorous and the pan may have to be removed from the heat so that a little extra liquid can be beaten in to thin it. A balloon whisk or coiled wire whisk is a useful implement for making a roux-based sauce.

After the liquid has been incorporated, the sauce is simmered to bring it to maximum thickness and to take away the slightly raw taste of the flour.

Beurre Manié

This is another form of fat and flour thickening, this time to be added to sauces that are already cooked, typically stews or poaching liquids.

Equal quantities of soft butter and flour are blended together to form a smooth, thick paste. Small pieces of the paste are whisked gradually into the simmering liquid and the sauce is cooked, whisking or stirring vigorously all the time, until the butter gradually melts and releases the flour.

Cornflour Sauces and Other Slaked Thickenings

These are fairly basic and not difficult to prepare. A thickening agent, such as cornflour, is mixed with a little cold liquid to form a smooth paste – a process known as slaking. Then a little of the hot liquid is stirred in before combining the paste with the remaining hot liquid. The sauce is then cooked over medium heat and stirred continuously until it boils.

Although ordinary flour is sometimes used (for example, to thicken a casserole), fine starch thickenings are more popular. The culinary term for these is *fécules* and they are produced by washing the starch to achieve a fine, light texture. The most common thickening agent in this type of sauce is cornflour. This gives a slightly gelatinous texture to the sauce, and it contributes a very mild flavour and an opaque appearance to clear liquids. A cornflour sauce should be simmered gently for 3–5 minutes after boiling in order to reach maximum thickness.

Arrowroot is another popular thickening agent, particularly for making sweet sauces and fruit glazes. This is because, unlike cornflour, arrowroot clears as it boils, so the sauce will not look opaque. Furthermore, it is tasteless, so it does not affect the flavour of delicate sauces. Another important characteristic of arrowroot is that it reaches its maximum thickness at boiling point and should not be cooked beyond this stage. If the sauce is allowed to simmer it will become thinner.

Potato flour and rice flour are two other fine starches which may be slaked and incorporated with a sauce, but they are less commonly used.

Liaison Sauces

These sauces highlight the magic of chemistry, as two liquids that normally repel each other come together in a creamy liaison. A fat, such as butter or oil, and a liquid, such as wine or vinegar, form an emulsion which is stabilized by the presence of an additional ingredient such as egg yolks.

Typical examples of liaisons, or emulsions, include mayonnaise, hollandaise and béarnaise sauces. The consistency depends on the quantity of egg yolk and fat and, in the case of cooked sauces such as hollandaise, the careful monitoring of the temperature at which the emulsion is prepared.

Great care and attention is required when making these sauces – if the balance is thrown by adding the ingredients too quickly, trying to incorporate too much fat, overheating, or not whisking enough, curdling will result and this spells disaster.

However, a curdled emulsion can be rescued by carefully starting again. A fresh egg yolk should be used and the curdled sauce should then be incorporated drop by drop.

When the sauce is completed, a wide range of flavourings may be added.

Egg Sauces

Because of their slow setting properties and rich flavour, egg yolks are a classic ingredient for enriching sauces and helping them to thicken slightly. Egg sauces are usually richer and more temperamental than ones that include some form of starch, and the cooking process must be gentle to avoid curdling.

For a custard-type sauce, the yolks are beaten lightly to break them down and the liquid for the sauce is heated, but not boiled, before being added to the yolks. The mixture is then cooked very gently in a double boiler or in a saucepan over hot water until there is slight evidence of thickening. If the sauce is cooked over too high a heat or for too long, the egg yolks will begin to set more firmly and separate out, causing the mixture to curdle. If a sauce of this type curdles it cannot be rescued.

Egg yolks can also be added to a sauce by combining them with a little of the hot liquid then stirring them in, or by mixing them with cream. In these instances their role is to enrich the sauce rather than to thicken it.

Egg yolks are often combined with starch to provide a more stable thickening and to enrich a sauce. The classic example is confectioner's custard, which relies on flour for the main thickening but incorporates egg yolks for richness. The flour stabilizes the egg yolk and milk mixture so it can be boiled until very thick. The proportion of flour to liquid is very high in this mixture, and if the flour is not boiled it will not thicken or taste cooked. Sauces that incorporate a very small amount of cornflour are not necessarily sufficiently stable to be heated to a high temperature.

Other Thickeners

Puréed vegetables and fruit, grains, pulses, bread, ground nuts, blood and liver are all examples of ingredients used to thicken sauces. Vegetables are popular in light, low-fat sauces, especially root ones such as carrots, parsnips and potatoes. Grains, beans and pulses thicken a sauce by absorbing and reducing the liquid content and imparting some of their starch to the remaining liquid. Bread acts in much the same way, only more so, by swelling and absorbing liquid, then breaking down and thickening the sauce. Nuts are less powerful as thickeners, but they do provide flavour and enrich the mixture.

Blood and liver both contribute their own distinctive characteristics. Dishes thickened with blood are known as "jugged" and the blood reacts in the same way as egg yolks – if it is overcooked the sauce will curdle and separate. Also, precautions have to be taken to prevent the blood from coagulating after it is drawn from the animal – it must not be exposed to air and a little acid in the form of vinegar is usually added.

MARINADES

These often form the basis of a sauce or become part of the sauce in a finished dish. A marinade is a flavouring mixture in which ingredients are soaked before they are cooked. The marinating time can be anything from as little as 30 minutes for delicate foods such as fish, to several days for meat and game. Long marinating can only be carried out on foods that are absolutely fresh, otherwise there is a danger of spoilage and even food poisoning.

Macerating is the equivalent term for the preparation of sweet ingredients primarily fruit. Alcohol (a wine or liqueur) is added with sugar to extract the juice from the fruit.

There are three types of marinades: cooked, raw and dry mixtures. The first two are relevant to this book, the dry type being more applicable to the use of herbs and spices.

One of the most common ingredients for a cooked marinade is red wine. The wine is cooked with flavouring ingredients then cooled completely before being poured over the food to be marinated – usually poultry, meat or game. The food must be covered and chilled if it is to be marinated for any length of time.

Raw marinades generally use lighter ingredients, such as citrus juice or white wine. Sometimes the raw marinade may replace the cooking process; for example *seviche* is a dish of raw white fish which is marinated in lime juice. The lime juice causes the delicate protein in the fish to become firm and white, just as it does when it is cooked.

STOCKS

It is well worth making your own stock, as it is superior in flavour to stock cubes and concentrates and is useful for both sauce and soup making. Make a large quantity and freeze it in convenient amounts. Sometimes wine is added, but this can give a metallic flavour.

Fish Stock

MAKES 600–750 ML/1–1¼ PT

225 g/8 oz white fish trimmings (heads and bones)
6 white peppercorns
1 small onion, sliced
1 stick celery, cut into 3
Sprig of parsley
Sprig of thyme
1 small bay leaf

Wash the fish trimmings and place in a saucepan with the remaining ingredients. Cover with cold water and bring to simmering point. Remove any scum that comes to the surface. Cover and simmer for about 1 hour.

STRAIN AND USE AS REQUIRED OR COOL QUICKLY AND FREEZE IN A SUITABLE CONTAINER.

Vegetable Stock

This is an ideal way of using up vegetables, but avoid very strong-flavoured vegetables or ones that could cause the stock to become cloudy, such as parsnip. Another way of making vegetable stock is to keep the water that vegetables have been cooked in.

MAKES ABOUT 900 ML/1½ PT

350 g/12 oz mixed vegetables, such as celery, carrot, watercress stalks, tomato, mushroom peelings or leeks
4 white peppercorns
Bouquet garni, made of parsley, thyme, bay leaf
Salt and pepper

Rinse the vegetables under cold water. Put in a saucepan with the peppercorns, herbs and a pinch of salt, then cover with about 1 l/1¾ pt cold water. Bring slowly to the boil, reduce the heat, then cover and simmer gently for about 1½ hours. Strain, then remove the stock to the pan and reduce over high heat to get a more concentrated stock. Add seasoning to taste.

USE STRAIGHT AWAY OR COOL QUICKLY AND FREEZE IN SUITABLE CONTAINERS.

Chicken Stock

Raw or cooked bones may be used, but be careful that cooked bones have not become stale. Duck or turkey bones can be used in the same way.

MAKES ABOUT 1 L/1¾ PT

Bones from one carcass
1 onion, sliced
1 carrot, sliced
Piece of leek (optional)
6 peppercorns
Bouquet garni made of parsley, thyme and bay leaf

Break the carcass into pieces, place in a large saucepan and add all the remaining ingredients, plus cold water to cover. Bring slowly to the boil, skimming off any foam that comes to the surface. Cover and simmer for about 1½ hours.

STRAIN AND USE IMMEDIATELY, OR COOL QUICKLY AND FREEZE IN SUITABLE CONTAINERS.

Brown Stock

The best-flavoured stock is made from bones with a bit of meat left on them. Have the bones cut into suitable sizes.

MAKES ABOUT 1 L/1¾ PT

1¼ kg/2½ lb shin of beef bones, cut into pieces
1 Spanish onion, sliced
2 carrots, sliced
2 sticks celery, cut into 3
Sprig of parsley
Sprig of thyme
1 bay leaf
6 black peppercorns
Salt

Roast the bones in a hot oven until brown, to extract the fat. This process is important as it adds to the richness and colour of the stock. It may take longer depending on the size of the bones; add a little dripping if necessary. Transfer the bones to a large saucepan.

Add the vegetables, stir and cook until just coloured. Pour on 2½ l/4 pt cold water and bring slowly to the boil, skimming to remove any scum. Add the herbs, peppercorns and a little salt. Cover the pan and simmer gently for about 3 hours. Remove the bones and vegetables then reduce the liquid if a more concentrated stock is required.

STRAIN, THEN USE IMMEDIATELY OR COOL QUICKLY AND FREEZE IN SUITABLE CONTAINERS.

OTHER STOCKS AND THEIR USES

WHITE STOCK

Made from a mixture of bones, but not mutton, lamb and ham bones as they are a bit strong for a several purpose stock, plus the usual vegetables. Delicate on flavour; use for cream soups, white sauces and aspic. The stronger lamb stock is good for Scotch broth, lamb casseroles and gravy.

GAME STOCK

This is a brown stock made from game carcasses and beef bones. It can be made from the second cooking of beef bones, plus the usual vegetables and herbs. Use with game, pies, pâtés and casseroles.

HOUSEHOLD STOCK

A general-purpose white stock made from ham bones, lamb, veal or chicken plus any raw trimmings. Bacon rinds are also ideal, plus the usual vegetables and herbs. For use in simple casseroles, sauces and soups.

MEAT GLAZE

This is made from brown stock and is used to enrich sauces. It can be stored in the refrigerator for a short time or frozen in small quantities, and is well worth making as it gives sauces a really professional finish.

Strain some brown stock and make sure it is completely grease free. Place in a large pan and boil rapidly, uncovered. Skim when necessary. When the stock has reduced sufficiently it will become syrupy. Pour it into a jar or suitable freezer container and store until required. See Madeira sauce (page 33).

ASPIC

This deserves special mention as it cannot be overlooked in a book on sauces. Aspic is a clear coating which is applied to food to enhance its appearance and prevent it from drying out, as well as to contribute to the flavour.

Aspic jelly is made from a full-flavoured stock, sometimes enriched with wine, and clarified until sparkling then set with gelatine. Sometimes the natural setting properties of meat, fish or chicken are enough to set the aspic but it is usual to add extra gelatine to be sure of success. It is important to follow the instructions for clarifying stock closely, making sure all equipment is completely clean and grease free.

Sometimes aspic is combined with a béchamel, mayonnaise or espagnole sauce to make a chaudfroid sauce for coating cold meats or fish.

Aspic Jelly

This should be sufficient to add to a chaudfroid sauce and for setting over the decoration. Use over chicken, meat, fish, eggs and canapés. Scald all the equipment with boiling water before making the aspic jelly.

MAKES 1 L/1¾ PT

900 ml/1½ pt good strong stock
175 ml/6 fl oz sherry and water mixed
2 tbsp white wine or cider vinegar
40 g/1½ oz gelatine, soaked in a little of the measured stock
2 egg whites and their shells, crushed

Put the cold stock in a large, grease-free, spotlessly clean saucepan. Stir in the sherry and water, wine or vinegar and gelatine. Heat gently to dissolve the gelatine.

To clarify the stock, whisk the egg whites until frothy then add to the stock with the egg shells, still heating gently. Continue whisking until the liquid is just below boiling point. A thick crust will form on the top. Remove the pan from the heat to allow the foam or crust to subside then repeat twice more; the liquid should become clear. Remove any foam, being careful not to break it up.

Place a large piece of scalded muslin into a large, clean sieve, place this over a clean, grease-free bowl and very carefully strain the liquid. The aspic should be quite clear. If not scald everything again and strain again.

IT IS POSSIBLE TO FREEZE ASPIC, BUT NOT IF IT HAS BECOME CLOUDY, UNLESS YOU ONLY PLAN TO ADD IT TO A SAUCE.

CHAPTER TWO

From Saucepan to Sauceboat

~

MANY SAUCES DETERIORATE from good beginnings to an inferior condition when served. It is important to distinguish between those sauces that can be cooked ahead and kept hot or reheated and others that have to be served straight away.

Keeping Sauces Hot

Sauces thickened with starch can usually be kept hot for a limited period or they can be cooled, chilled and reheated successfully. Enriching ingredients that may curdle, such as cream, fromage frais, yogurt or egg yolks, should not be added until after the sauce has been reheated. Always remember that sauces should not be kept warm for long periods as this may encourage bacterial growth which could result in food poisoning. They should be kept hot by placing them over a pan of hot water or in a bain marie.

Press cling film or dampened greaseproof paper all over the surface of milk sauces or custards to prevent a skin forming. Dampening the greaseproof paper stops it from sticking. Gravies and lighter sauces thickened with flour will only form a light skin, so covering them with a close-fitting lid is sufficient. Whisk or stir them well before serving.

It is important to prevent a sauce from overcooking while it is kept hot. If you can't reduce the heat enough to keep the sauce hot without simmering, then stand the saucepan in a roasting tin of hot water or pour the sauce into a bowl and place it over a saucepan of hot water.

Cooked liaison sauces can only be kept warm for a short time while the finishing touches are added to the main dish. Do not attempt to keep hollandaise or béarnaise sauces and their sister recipes hot as they quickly thicken and become inferior in texture; worse, there is a danger of separation.

Cooling, Chilling and Freezing Sauces

Sauces thickened with starch or puréed vegetables generally keep well in the refrigerator or freezer but do not add cream, eggs or other enriching agents until you want to use the sauce. The sauce should be poured into a cold airtight container as soon as it is cooked and the surface covered to prevent a skin forming. Cool as quickly as possible then chill. Milk sauces keep for 1–2 days in the refrigerator; gravies and wine sauces will keep for 2–3 days.

If the sauce is to be frozen, it should be placed in the freezer as soon as it is cold. Remember to label the container with notes on any enriching ingredients that have to be added on reheating.

Thawing and Reheating Sauces

Frozen sauces should be thawed in the freezer container until soft. Sauces thickened with starch will look lumpy and slightly separated when they have thawed but they will return to normal if they are thoroughly whisked. Some sauces tend to be slightly thinner on thawing, and thick-set mixtures based on cornflour or arrowroot will become significantly more liquid after freezing and thawing.

Reheat the sauce fairly gently, stirring or whisking all the time, then bring the mixture to the boil just before serving. Add any flavouring ingredients and taste for seasoning.

Serving Sauces

Always heat sauceboats, jugs or dishes before pouring in hot sauce. One practical method is to fill the vessel with boiling water from the kettle and set it aside, then drain and dry it just before filling. Stand the vessel on a saucer or plate to catch drips. Serving a sauce from a dish with a small ladle can be an attractive method.

If the sauce is poured over food, take care not to drown it. Instead, just partly coat it and offer the rest of the sauce separately. Remember to clean the edges of a serving dish or individual plate of any drips after adding the sauce and before taking it to the table, as messy dishes look most unattractive.

Special Effects

Many decorative effects can be achieved when serving sauces. For example, instead of pouring the sauce over the food, try flooding the plate with sauce carefully placing the food on top of it.

A particularly effective presentation is to serve two sauces together on the same plate. The sauces, savoury or sweet, hot or cold, must have complementary colours and flavours, and should also complement the food, of course. Try any of the following presentations, but note that you need to work quickly, and that for hot sauces the plate must be well heated and the food piping hot.

- Separate areas of the plate can be flooded with two different sauces that meet in the middle. Both sauces must be the same consistency and the plate must be held level.
- A central puddle of sauce can be surrounded by an outer ring of contrasting sauce and the two lightly feathered into each other with a cocktail stick where they meet.
- One sauce can be thinly flooded on the plate and the second sauce randomly trickled over, then marbled through with a cocktail stick.
- Small dots of sauce can be dropped into a flooded plate of sauce then feathered or marbled into distinctive patterns by dragging a cocktail stick through the dots.

USEFUL TIPS FOR SAUCE SUCCESS

- Never rush the process of sauce making. Good sauces are the result of time and care. Whenever possible, use home-made stock; if not, be selective about bought alternatives. Stock cubes vary enormously in quality – some are very powerful and destroy delicate flavours. Chilled prepared stock, available from the chiller cabinet in large supermarkets, is a better alternative for special sauces.
- Select the right-sized pan for the quantity of sauce being made. A heavy-based pan with good conduction properties gives the best control. Use a suitable-sized mixing spoon or whisk but remember not to use a metal whisk in a non-stick pan.
- Add any liquid gradually, especially when there is a danger of lumps forming.
- Cook the sauce slowly to "cook out" the taste of the flour.
- Large proportions of acid can inhibit thickening, so the quantity of starch should be increased accordingly. This is only relevant when making a vinegar-rich sauce, for example in pickles.
- Cheese, concentrated tomato purée, *beurre manié*, egg yolks and blood cause a sauce to thicken further on cooling slightly – be aware of this if you intend serving a sauce warm or cold.
- Seasonings and flavouring ingredients should be added in stages when preparing some sauces. For example, a sauce that is simmered for a long period or reduced by boiling should not be seasoned to taste until after it is cooked, as the flavour will be more concentrated at the end of the cooking time. This is mainly relevant to salt, pepper and other strong flavours but also applies to sharpening ingredients, such as lemon juice, or sweeteners, such as sugar.
- If a starch-thickened sauce becomes lumpy, remove the pan from the heat and whisk the mixture vigorously. If this does not work, strain the sauce through a fine sieve, pressing it through, then return it to the heat and simmer until reduced if it is too thin. If the sauce is too thick, more liquid may be added to thin it. Remember to whisk or stir in the liquid to avoid a repeat performance of sieving out lumps!

CHAPTER THREE

Foundation Sauces

~

Basic White

This recipe is for a pouring sauce. See the chart for additional flavourings.

MAKES 600 ML/1 PT

40 g/1½ oz butter or margarine
40 g/1½ oz plain flour
600 ml/1 pt milk, slightly warm
Salt and pepper

Melt the butter or margarine in a medium-sized heavy-based saucepan. Stir in the flour to make a roux and mix well with a wooden spoon. Cook, stirring, for 1 minute.

Remove the pan from the heat and stir in a little of the milk, then return the pan to the heat, stirring until the mixture thickens. Continue gradually adding the milk like this until it is all used up. Giving the sauce a good beat in between each addition of milk results in a smooth glossy sauce.

When all the milk has been added, bring the mixture to the boil, reduce the heat and simmer for about 5 minutes to make sure the flour is cooked. Add seasoning and any other flavouring.

SERVE STRAIGHT AWAY OR COOL AND FREEZE.

Béchamel

This is a basic white sauce but the milk is flavoured with vegetables and herbs.

MAKES 600 ML/1 PT

600 ml/1 pt milk
1 small onion, peeled
6 cloves
Blade of mace or pinch of ground mace
4 peppercorns
1 small carrot
1 bay leaf
Sprig of parsley
40 g/1½ oz butter
40 g/1½ oz plain flour
Salt and pepper

Pour the milk into a saucepan. Stick the onion with the cloves and add to the milk with the mace, peppercorns, carrot, bay leaf and parsley. Leave on a low heat for 10–15 minutes but do not allow it to boil. Remove the pan from the heat and leave to stand for 15 minutes for the flavours to infuse, then strain, discarding the vegetables and herbs.

Proceed with the remaining ingredients as for basic white sauce, using the warm milk.

THIS WILL FREEZE WITH A PIECE OF CLING FILM ON TOP TO PREVENT A SKIN FORMING.

Simple Brown

This basic brown sauce is a pouring sauce, with a quick cooking time. Use home-made stock or good quality commercial stock. Serve with liver, lamb, pork or chicken.

MAKES 600 ML/1 PT

25 g/1 oz lard or dripping
1 small carrot, diced
1 onion, chopped
25 g/1 oz plain flour
600 ml/1 pt good strong stock
Salt and pepper

Melt the lard or dripping in a saucepan and sauté the carrot and onion over a low heat for about 10 minutes until the onion is softened and lightly browned.

Stir in the flour, lower the heat and cook very gently, stirring, so the roux turns a golden brown. Gradually stir in the stock and bring to the boil, stirring, until the sauce thickens. Add seasoning to taste. Strain into a warm sauceboat.

WILL FREEZE WELL.

BASIC VARIATIONS for 300 ml/½ pt white sauce

NAME	RECIPE	SUITABLE STOCKS	USES
Anchovy	2 tsp anchovy essence or 1 tin mashed anchovies with a few fillets chopped.	½ milk and ½ fish stock	Baked, steamed or grilled fish, fish pie.
Anchovy and Egg	2 tsp anchovy essence and 1 hard-boiled egg, chopped.	All milk.	Poured over eggs or baked fish steaks, fish pie.
Cheese	50 g/2 oz strong Cheddar, grated.	All milk, or ½ milk and ½ vegetable stock.	Vegetables, fish, pasta and eggs.
Egg	1–2 hard-boiled eggs, chopped.	All milk.	Vegetables, fish.
Egg and Parsley	1 hard-boiled egg and 1 tbsp fresh chopped parsley	All milk or ½ milk and ½ vegetable stock.	Gammon and boiled bacon, vegetables.
Fennel	2 tbsp chopped fennel, slightly cooked.	All milk or ½ milk and ½ vegetable stock.	Fish and other vegetables.
Parsley	1–2 tbsp chopped fresh parsley.	All milk, ½ milk and ½ fish stock, or ½ milk and ½ vegetable stock.	Vegetables, fish, bacon, chicken or rabbit.
Mushroom	125 g/4 oz button mushrooms, sliced and cooked in 25 g/1 oz butter.	All milk and 1 tbsp cream, if liked.	Chicken, fish and vegetables.

Espagnole

This is the foundation of many rich sauces. It takes time, so it is worth making quite a lot then freezing it in 300 ml/½ pt or 600 ml/1 pt quantities.

MAKES 600 ML/1 PT

50 g/2 oz lean bacon rashers, chopped
50 g /2 oz butter or dripping
1 small onion, chopped
1 small carrot, finely diced
1 shallot, sliced
50 g/2 oz plain flour
600 ml/1 pt good brown stock
4 mushrooms, or mushroom stalks and peelings
Bouquet garni
1 tbsp tomato purée
1 tbsp sherry (optional)
Salt and pepper

Sauté the bacon in the butter or dripping. Add the prepared vegetables and fry them gently without browning for about 3–5 minutes.

Stir in the flour and cook slowly so the flour gradually browns and becomes a good russet colour; this can take up to 30 minutes if done properly. Stir occasionally, and take care not to scorch the roux, as this would ruin the flavour.

Gradually stir in the stock, add the mushrooms and bouquet garni, then bring to the boil, stirring. Remove any scum and simmer gently for 30 minutes.

Add the tomato purée, sherry if using, and seasoning. Simmer for a further 10–15 minutes.

Strain the sauce by pounding through some of the vegetables and discard the remnants. Taste and adjust seasoning. Reheat the sauce gently.

IDEAL FOR FREEZING.

VARIATION

Demi-glace

This is espagnole sauce with extra strong stock added for flavour. Make the espagnole sauce. 20 minutes before the end of cooking time add about 150 ml/¼ pt extra strong stock and continue to cook to required consistency. A tablespoon of Madeira or sherry is often added at the end for added flavour.

Gravy

Gravy is most frequently made in a roasting tin from the juices left after roasting meat or poultry. It may be either thick or thin.

Thick Gravy

MAKES 300 ML/½ PT

2 tbsp of pan juices from roasting a joint or bird
1 tbsp plain flour
300 ml/½ pt meat stock or vegetable water and good quality commercial stock
Salt and pepper

Pour off most of the fat from the roasting pan to leave the 2 tbsp required. Over a low heat, blend the flour in with the fat, using a spoon. Cook for a few minutes to allow the roux to brown without scorching. Gradually stir in the stock, bring to boiling point and cook for 2–3 minutes. Season to taste, strain and serve hot with the roast.

Thin Gravy

This is best with beef.

MAKES 300 ML/½ PT

Pan juices from roasting a joint of meat
300 ml/½ pt meat stock or vegetable water and good quality commercial stock

Pour away all the fat from the roasting tin, add the hot stock and stir well. Bring to the boil and reduce for 2–3 minutes.

Fresh Tomato

This is well worth making and freezing when there is a glut of tomatoes in the summer but it may also be made with canned tomatoes, which have a stronger flavour. It goes well with meat, fish, pasta and vegetable dishes.

MAKES ABOUT 450 ML/¾ PT

1 onion, chopped
50 g/2 oz streaky bacon, chopped
1 carrot, diced
2 tbsp oil
3 tbsp flour
675 g/1½ lb fresh tomatoes, chopped
200 ml/7 fl oz vegetable stock
1 bay leaf
Sprig of parsley
2 fresh basil leaves, crushed
Salt and pepper
Pinch of sugar (optional)

Place the onion, bacon and carrot in a saucepan with the oil. Heat gently and cook for about 5 minutes.

Stir in the flour and cook for about 2 minutes, then stir in all the remaining ingredients and bring to the boil. Cover and cook gently for 1 hour, stirring occasionally.

Allow to cool slightly then sieve the sauce, taste and adjust the seasoning. Add a pinch of sugar if the sauce is too acid.

REHEAT IF USING STRAIGHT AWAY OR FREEZE IN A RIGID PLASTIC CONTAINER.

Velouté

This is a reduced white sauce with cream added.

MAKES 300 ML/½ PT

25 g/1 oz butter
25 g/1 oz plain flour
600 ml/1 pt white stock
Mushroom trimmings
Parsley stalks
1–2 tbsp single or double cream
Salt and pepper

Melt the butter then add the flour and cook the roux, stirring, for 2 minutes. Gradually add the stock, stirring, and bring to the boil. Add the mushroom trimmings and parsley stalks.

Simmer gently for about 1 hour until reduced by half. Strain and return to the rinsed-out saucepan.

Stir in the cream, season to taste and reheat gently. For a richer sauce, add a knob of butter at the end. For a richer sauce still, finish with an egg liaison and extra cream.

FREEZE THIS SAUCE BEFORE ADDING THE CREAM.

Bread

Roast chicken calls out for this sauce – it's just not the same without it.

MAKES 300 ML/½ PT

300 ml/½ pt milk
1 onion
6 cloves
Piece of mace or pinch of ground mace
1 bay leaf
50 g/2 oz fresh breadcrumbs
Knob of butter
Salt and freshly ground black pepper
A little cream (optional)

Pour the milk into a saucepan. Peel the onion and stick in the cloves, then put it in the milk with the mace and bay leaf. Bring almost to the boil. Remove the pan from the heat and infuse for 30 minutes.

Remove the onion, bay leaf and mace and stir in the breadcrumbs. Heat gently then add the butter and cook until the sauce comes together and looks creamy.

Season to taste and add the cream, if using. If the sauce thickens too much or catches, thin it with a little extra milk.

WILL FREEZE.

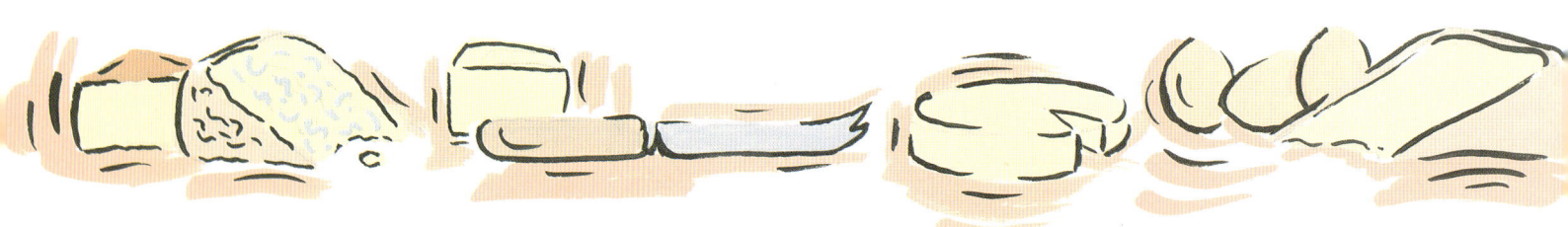

Egg Custard

Traditional egg custard relies on egg yolks to thicken it, and the more egg yolks the richer the sauce will be. This sauce can be used as a base for ice cream.

MAKES ABOUT 600 ML/1 PT

450 ml/¾ pt milk
A vanilla pod
5 egg yolks
50 g/2 oz sugar

Put the milk in a saucepan with the vanilla pod and warm; do not boil.

Put the egg yolks in a bowl with the sugar and whisk together until thick and creamy. Remove vanilla pod and stir in the hot milk. Rinse the saucepan, pour in the custard and return to the heat.

Heat very gently, stirring continuously, until the custard thickens. Doing this too quickly could cause the custard to curdle. The custard is the correct consistency when it coats the back of the spoon.

NOT SUITABLE FOR FREEZING.

VARIATION

Infuse the milk with lemon or orange rind. Add 1 tbsp Tia Maria or rum to the custard.

Red or White Wine

There are two ways of making a wine sauce: either make a roux and use half wine and half stock for the liquid, or cook wine or a marinade with stock, then reduce and thicken it with a *beurre manié*. This sauce is made by the latter method.

MAKES 900 ML/1½ PT

1 tbsp each of chopped onion, carrot and celery
25 g/1 oz butter
600 ml/1 pt red or white wine
300 ml/½ pt good stock – chicken stock if using white wine, beef stock if using red wine
1 small bay leaf
Salt and pepper
50 g/2 oz beurre manié (see page 7)

Lightly sauté the vegetables in the butter, then stir in the wine, stock and bay leaf. Bring to the boil, then simmer until reduced by half. Season to taste. Thicken with the *beurre manié*.

WILL FREEZE.

Hollandaise

Hollandaise, béarnaise and mayonnaise are liaison sauces. They require time and practice since they can easily curdle. This is because a high proportion of butter or oil is added to egg yolks which need time to absorb the fat. Too much heat will cook the egg yolk and prevent this process. With careful handling the fat is absorbed and the egg is cooked. This sauce is served warm, usually with salmon or asparagus.

MAKES ABOUT 300 ML/½ PT

1 tbsp lemon juice or vinegar
1 tsp water
2 egg yolks
150 g/5 oz butter, softened
Salt and pepper

Place the lemon juice or vinegar and water in a bowl that fits over a pan of simmering water. Make sure the base of the bowl doesn't touch the water.

Beat the egg yolks and add them to the bowl with a knob of the butter. Whisk well until a thick emulsion is formed and the whisk leaves a trail. Reduce the heat and gradually whisk in the remaining butter, then add seasoning to taste and extra lemon juice or vinegar if required. Beat well to give a glossy sauce. Serve immediately.

NOT SUITABLE FOR FREEZING.

Béarnaise

This is the same as hollandaise but is sharper. Serve with grilled steak.

MAKES 300 ML/½ PT

2 tbsp finely chopped shallots
4 peppercorns
50 ml/2 fl oz tarragon vinegar
50 ml/2 fl oz white wine vinegar
2 egg yolks
150 g/5 oz butter, softened
1 tbsp each of chopped fresh tarragon and chervil
Salt and pepper

Place the shallots, peppercorns and vinegars in a small saucepan. Bring to the boil, then boil to reduce to about 2 tbsp. Allow to cool slightly then proceed in the same way as for hollandaise, adding the herbs at the end with salt and pepper to taste.

NOT SUITABLE FOR FREEZING.

VARIATION

Choron

This is basic béarnaise sauce without the herbs. Stir in sufficient reduced fresh tomato pulp to give a good consistency – about 50 ml/2 fl oz to 300 ml/½ pt sauce. Or add about 2 tsp concentrated tomato purée.

Mayonnaise

This liaison sauce is the base for many variations. One of the traditional rules is to keep everything cool, but I always find that adding a little warm water works well and makes the sauce less sharp.

MAKES 150 ML/¼ PT

1 large egg yolk
Pinch each of salt, sugar, freshly ground pepper and dry mustard
150 ml/¼ pt good olive oil
1 tsp warm water
1 tbsp white wine vinegar, or to taste

Place the egg yolk in a bowl and blend in the seasonings. Beat in the oil drop by drop, whisking it well between each addition so it is completely absorbed each time and the mixture thickens.

When about half the oil has been added, gradually beat in the warm water. Once this has been included it is easier to add the remaining oil. When all the oil is mixed in, sharpen the flavour with vinegar to taste.

To save a curdled mayonnaise, start with a fresh egg yolk in a clean bowl and slowly beat in the curdled mixture. It may be necessary to add extra oil and vinegar as the sauce will be more eggy in flavour.

FREEZING NOT RECOMMENDED.

Chaudfroid

This sauce is prepared from one of several foundation sauces and can be made different colours for serving purposes. White chaudfroid is made from a béchamel or velouté; brown chaudfroid uses espagnole sauce. Mayonnaise chaudfroid can be made from mayonnaise, and it can also be coloured green, using spinach purée or herbs, or red, using tomato purée. The basic sauce should be the consistency of a coating sauce. Allow it to cool until it is thick enough to coat the food completely.

MAKES ABOUT 750 ML/1¼ PT

600 ml/1 pt béchamel or espagnole sauce (see page 17 or page 19)
4 sheets of gelatine or 2 tsp powdered gelatine
150 ml/¼ pt aspic jelly (see page 12)

The béchamel or espagnole sauce should be slightly warm with no lumps.

Dissolve the extra gelatine in the aspic jelly then stir into the sauce. When the sauce is thick enough, start coating the food. Keep an eye on the sauce in case it starts to set. If it does, place the pan in a little warm water.

FREEZE BASE SAUCE ONLY.

CHAPTER FOUR

Classic Sauces

~

Aurore

This is a coating sauce with tomato added, and can be used with fish, meat, eggs and vegetables. To give extra richness it should be "mounted" with extra butter.

MAKES 300 ML/½ PT

300 ml/½ pt béchamel sauce (see page 17)
1 tbsp tomato purée or 2 tbsp reduced thick fresh tomato pulp
50 g/2 oz unsalted butter
Salt and pepper

Make the béchamel in the usual way then stir in the tomato purée or fresh tomato pulp. Remove the pan from the heat.

Whisk in the butter a little at a time, do not return the pan to the heat after the butter has been added as it will separate out from the sauce. Taste and adjust the seasoning.

NOT SUITABLE FOR FREEZING.

Bercy

Serve this sauce with fish dishes.

MAKES 300 ML/½ PT

15 g/½ oz butter
2 shallots, finely chopped
150 ml/¼ pt dry white wine
300 ml/½ pt fish stock
1 tbsp lemon juice
Salt and freshly ground white pepper
25 g/1 oz beurre manié (see page 7)
1 tbsp chopped fresh parsley

Melt the butter in a small saucepan, add the onion and cook until soft, without browning. Add the wine, bring to the boil and cook until reduced by half.

Add the stock, lemon juice, salt and pepper. Return to the boil, simmer for 2 minutes then remove the pan from the heat.

Whisk in the *beurre manié* a little at a time with the parsley, then simmer for a few minutes until the sauce has thickened and is smooth. Taste and adjust the seasoning.

SUITABLE FOR FREEZING.

Chivry

This is a wonderful green sauce to serve with chicken, poached fish, vegetables and eggs.

MAKES 300 ML/½ PT

Bunch of chervil, tarragon and chives
125 g/4 oz fresh spinach, stalks removed
300 ml/½ pt velouté sauce or supreme sauce (see page 20 or page 29)
Small knob of butter (optional)
Pinch of freshly grated nutmeg (optional)

Wash the herbs and spinach. Cook these quickly in a little boiling water for about 5 minutes, then drain well and sieve. They should give about 1 tbsp purée.

Add this purée to the velouté or supreme sauce and heat through if necessary. An extra piece of butter may be added if using velouté sauce, and the nutmeg, if liked.

WILL FREEZE. THE PUREE OF HERBS AND SPINACH CAN BE PREPARED WHEN SEASONAL AND FROZEN IN ICE TRAYS.

CLASSIC SAUCES 25

Game

This is made with stock from game bones. Some wine may be added when making the stock, or use some marinade instead. Game sauce can be thickened with blood, which is obtained from the game from the butcher and should be mixed with vinegar to prevent it clotting. Stir the blood into the sauce to thicken it; never boil or it will separate.

MAKES 450 ML/¾ PT

2 tbsp oil
450 g/1 lb game bones
1 onion, chopped
1 clove garlic, crushed
1 carrot, cut in large pieces
1 stick celery, cut in large pieces
300 ml/½ pt red wine or marinade
600 ml/1 pt water
1 bay leaf ⎫
6 juniper berries ⎬ leave these out if using the marinade
4 peppercorns ⎭
75 g/3 oz beurre manié (see page 7)
2 tbsp redcurrant jelly
Salt and pepper

Heat the oil in a large pan and brown the bones and vegetables. Add the wine, water and spices, if using, cover and simmer for at least 30 minutes. Strain, return to the pan, and simmer until reduced to 450 ml/¾ pt.

Gradually blend in the *beurre manié* to thicken, then bring to the boil, reduce the heat and simmer for 5 minutes. Stir in the redcurrant jelly and adjust the seasoning.

PERFECT FOR FREEZING.

Rich Prawn Sauce with Dill

This sauce is well worth the effort of making it. Serve over fish or scallops, or use as part of a filling for pancakes or over an omelette.

MAKES 300 ML/½ PT

175 g/6 oz fresh cooked prawns in their shells
5 tbsp single cream
40 g/1½ oz butter
3 tbsp plain flour
300 ml/½ pt fish or chicken stock
2 egg yolks
1 tbsp lemon juice
2 tbsp chopped fresh dill
Salt and freshly ground white pepper

Wash the prawns, remove the shells and place the shells in a saucepan with the cream. Bring to the boil, then remove from the heat, leave to infuse for about 10 minutes, and strain.

Melt the butter in a pan, stir in the flour and cook for 2 minutes, stirring continuously to prevent it from catching. Gradually add the stock and bring to the boil, stirring. Simmer for 2–3 minutes.

Remove the sauce from the heat. Blend the egg yolks with the cream then gradually add to the sauce with the lemon juice, dill, prawns, salt and pepper. Reheat gently without boiling.

NOT SUITABLE FOR FREEZING.

Beurre Blanc

This classic French sauce is served with poached fish.

MAKES ABOUT 175 ML/6 FL OZ

1 shallot or small onion, finely chopped
2 tbsp white wine vinegar
Salt and freshly ground white pepper
150 g/5 oz unsalted butter, softened

Place the shallot or onion and the vinegar in a small saucepan, season with salt and pepper and cook over a fairly high heat until reduced by a quarter.

Add a quarter of the butter, beat well with a wire whisk and bring to the boil, then quickly remove from the heat and gradually whisk in the remaining butter a little at a time.

The sauce should thicken to the consistency of thin mayonnaise.

SAUCE IS QUICK TO MAKE SO THERE IS NO NEED TO FREEZE IT.

Basic Curry Sauce

This a basic recipe to serve with vegetables, fish, chicken or eggs. For an authentic Indian curry sauce see page 49.

MAKES 600 ML/1 PT

50 g/2 oz creamed coconut
450 ml/¾ pt hot water
1 onion, chopped
1 clove garlic, crushed
4 tbsp oil
2 tbsp curry powder
2 tbsp plain flour
1 carrot, grated
225 g/8 oz can chopped tomatoes
1 tbsp tomato purée
½ tsp salt

Place the coconut in a measuring jug and add some of the hot water. Break up the coconut then stir in the remaining water and leave to infuse.

Put the onion and garlic in a saucepan with the oil and cook gently for about 5 minutes until softened. Add the curry powder, stir well and cook for 5 minutes. Stir in the flour and cook for 3 minutes. Gradually add the coconut liquid. Stir in the remaining ingredients and bring to the boil. Simmer for 25 minutes.

USE WHEN REQUIRED OR FREEZE.

Bigarade

A slightly bitter sauce to serve with duck and other game. Seville oranges are best, but since they are not available all year round you can use an ordinary orange and a little lemon juice to sharpen.

MAKES 450 ML/¾ PT

Rind and juice of 1 small orange
1 shallot, finely chopped
15 g/½ oz butter
150 ml/¼ pt red wine
300 ml/½ pt espagnole sauce (see page 19)
2 tsp redcurrant jelly
1 tbsp port (optional)
Lemon juice (optional)

Thinly shred the orange rind. Place it in a small pan of water, bring to the boil and cook for 5 minutes to soften. Refresh under cold water and keep on one side.

Place the shallot and butter in a small saucepan and cook until the shallot is soft, then add the wine. Reduce by about half, then stir in the espagnole sauce, orange juice, redcurrant jelly and port if using. Cook for about 5 minutes. Strain the sauce and stir in the reserved orange shreds, adding lemon juice to sharpen if necessary.

SUITABLE FOR FREEZING.

Caper

Serve with boiled lamb, mutton, chicken or plainly cooked fish. I always like to add a little chopped parsley but this is not traditional.

MAKES 600 ML/1 PT

40 g/1½ oz butter or margarine
40 g/1½ oz plain flour
600 ml/1 pt vegetable stock
2 tsp vinegar
½ tsp mustard
Salt and pepper
3 tbsp capers, slightly chopped
1–2 tbsp cream
1 tbsp chopped fresh parsley (optional)

Melt the butter or margarine in a pan, stir in the flour and cook for 2 minutes. Gradually add the stock, bring to the boil, stirring, and cook for 3 minutes.

Stir in the vinegar, mustard, salt, pepper and capers and cook for 2 minutes, then stir in the cream and the parsley, if using, taste, and adjust the seasoning if necessary.

THIS WILL FREEZE FOR A SHORT TIME.

Bordelaise

A gourmet sauce with bone marrow added. Serve with beef or game. Ask the butcher for pieces of marrow bone with the marrow left in.

MAKES 300 ML/½ PT

50 g/2 oz bone marrow, extracted from the bone
2 shallots, finely chopped
125 ml/4 fl oz red wine
300 ml/½ pt espagnole sauce (see page 19)
Freshly ground black pepper
Sprig of thyme
15 g/½ oz butter

Cut the raw marrow into slices and poach it gently for 1–2 minutes in a little stock or water. Remove with a slotted spoon and keep on one side.

Gently cook the shallots in the wine until softened and then reduce the wine by half. Stir in the espagnole sauce, a little pepper and thyme. Bring to the boil, stirring, then strain.

Add the marrow to the sauce and heat through, then remove from the heat and stir in the butter. Adjust the seasoning if necessary.

THIS WILL FREEZE FOR A SHORT TIME.

Smoked Salmon

This sauce is quick to prepare and goes well with most types of fish.

MAKES 450 ML/¾ PT

300 ml/½ pt fish stock
150 ml/¼ pt double cream
25 g/1 oz butter, softened
4 tsp cornflour
125 g/4 oz smoked salmon, chopped
2 tsp chopped fresh dill
Salt and pepper
1 tsp lemon juice (optional)

Place the fish stock and cream in a saucepan and bring to the boil, then reduce the heat.

Blend the butter and cornflour together and add to the sauce in pieces like a *beurre manié* (see page 7). Simmer for about 3 minutes, then stir in the smoked salmon, dill, salt and pepper to taste and the lemon juice if liked.

THIS WILL FREEZE BUT FOR A SHORT TIME ONLY.

Italienne

This is a useful sauce, and it always looks good when served poured over a sliced roast fillet of beef or a boned loin of lamb. It's also good with tongue.

MAKES 450 ML/¾ PT

1 shallot, finely chopped
125 ml/4 fl oz white wine
15 g/½ oz butter
50 g/2 oz button mushrooms, thinly sliced
50 g/2 oz cooked ham, cut into julienne strips
300 ml/½ pt demi-glace (see page 19)
2 tsp tomato purée
Chopped parsley

Place the shallot in a pan with the wine and butter and cook gently to soften the shallot and reduce the wine by half. Stir in the mushrooms, cook for 2 minutes, then add the ham, demi-glace, tomato purée and parsley. Cook for 5 minutes and serve poured over the meat.

THIS WILL FREEZE BUT THE HAM MIGHT DEVELOP A STALE FLAVOUR IF IT IS FROZEN FOR TOO LONG.

Bourguignonne

Beef can be cooked slowly in this rich wine sauce.

MAKES ABOUT 450 ML/¾ PT

25 g/1 oz butter
50 g/2 oz streaky bacon, chopped
1 small onion, chopped
1 small carrot, chopped
50 g/2 oz mushrooms, sliced
1 bay leaf
Sprig of parsley
Sprig of thyme
900 ml/1½ pt red wine
50 g/2 oz beurre manié (see page 7), or more if necessary
Salt and freshly ground black pepper

Melt the butter in a pan and fry the bacon and onion, until they are lightly browned and the onion is soft. Add the carrot, mushrooms, herbs and red wine. Bring to the boil and reduce by half. Remove the herbs.

Gradually add the *beurre manié*, whisking it in. Bring to the boil, still whisking, and cook for 3–4 minutes until thickened. Enrich with an extra 25 g/1 oz butter if liked.

THIS WILL FREEZE VERY WELL BUT NOT FOR MORE THAN 2 MONTHS.

Quick Beef and Mushroom

A quick and tasty sauce for serving with roast or grilled beef, or beef Wellington.

MAKES ABOUT 450 ML/¾ PT

1 small onion, finely chopped
15 g/½ oz butter
50 g/2 oz small button mushrooms, thinly sliced
295 g/10½ oz can condensed beef consommé
1 tbsp red wine vinegar
1½ tsp arrowroot
2 tbsp water

Place the onion and butter in a saucepan, cook gently to soften the onion then add the mushrooms and cook for about 3 minutes. Remove the pan from the heat.

Add the consommé and the vinegar. Blend the arrowroot with the water until smooth. Stir into the consommé, return the pan to the heat and cook until the sauce thickens and becomes clear.

NOT SUITABLE FOR FREEZING.

Charcutière

A sharp sauce to serve with meat, including rabbit and chicken.

MAKES ABOUT 300 ML/½ PT

1 small onion, finely chopped
25 g/1 oz butter
150 ml/¼ pt white wine
1 tbsp vinegar
50 g/2 oz gherkins, chopped
300 ml/½ pt espagnole sauce (see page 19)
½ tbsp French mustard, or to taste

Put the butter in a saucepan, add the onion and cook gently to soften without browning. Add the wine and vinegar. Reduce by half then stir in the remaining ingredients. Heat gently and cook for 2 minutes. Taste and add the mustard to balance the flavour.

WILL FREEZE FOR 1–2 MONTHS.

Poivrade

This is a well-flavoured, slightly piquant sauce. Serve with game or any marinated meat dish.

MAKES 300 ML/½ PT

1 tbsp oil
1 small onion, chopped
1 small carrot, chopped
Sprig of parsley
1 small bay leaf
4 tbsp red wine
2 tbsp red wine vinegar
2 tbsp butter
2 tbsp plain flour
600 ml/1 pt good strong stock
1 tbsp black peppercorns, crushed
Salt and pepper

Heat the oil in a pan, add the vegetables and herbs and cook for 5 minutes to soften without browning. Add the wine and vinegar and cook until reduced by half. Keep on one side.

In a clean saucepan, make a roux with the butter and flour and cook until brown. Gradually pour in the stock, stirring then bring to the boil, add the cooked vegetables and their liquor and simmer for 30 minutes. Add the peppercorns and seasoning and simmer for a further 10 minutes, then strain.

Return the sauce to the rinsed-out pan and continue cooking until the required consistency is achieved; it should be a good pouring sauce.

SUITABLE FOR FREEZING.

Supreme

A velouté sauce made with chicken stock and enriched with cream and meat jelly. It is usually served with chicken or rabbit or used as a base for chaudfroid.

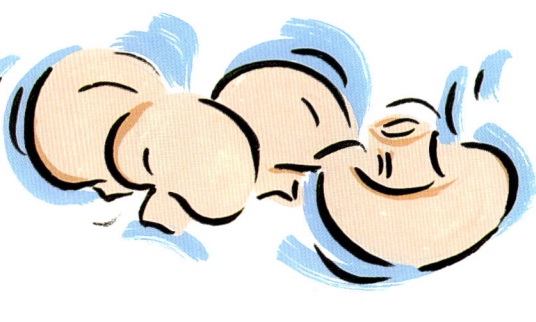

MAKES ABOUT 450 ML/¾ PT

300 ml/½ pt velouté sauce (see page 20)
125 ml/4 fl oz double cream
3 tbsp butter

Heat the velouté sauce if necessary, then stir in the cream and butter. Heat very gently for a few minutes, then strain and serve.

NOT SUITABLE FOR FREEZING.

Onion Cream (Soubise)

A deliciously smooth creamy sauce to serve with lamb, egg or vegetable dishes. Some of the stock could be replaced with white wine.

MAKES 450 ML/¾ PT

25 g/1 oz butter
2 tbsp oil
175 g/6 oz Spanish onions, finely diced
1 medium onion, finely sliced
1 small clove garlic, crushed
3 tbsp plain flour
300 ml/½ pt chicken or vegetable stock, warmed
150 ml/¼ pt single cream
Salt and freshly ground white pepper
1 tsp lemon juice

Heat the butter and oil in a pan and stir in the onions. Cover with a damp piece of greaseproof paper, put the lid on the pan and leave to cook gently until softened but not browned, about 10–15 minutes.

Add the garlic and flour and cook for 1 minute, stirring. Gradually stir in the stock and cream, then cook over a low heat for 10 minutes.

Sieve or liquidize the sauce. Return it to the pan, add the seasoning and lemon juice and heat gently.

NOT SUITABLE FOR FREEZING.

Cumberland

A lovely sauce to serve with ham, tongue, pork and turkey. You can make it richer by adding more redcurrant jelly and a tablespoon of Grand Marnier. It is a good idea to make the sauce in advance so it matures.

MAKES 450 ML/¾ PT

1 lemon
1 orange
225 g/8 oz redcurrant jelly
50 ml/2 fl oz port
2 tsp arrowroot
1 tbsp Grand Marnier (optional)

Thinly peel the rind from the lemon and the orange and cut it into very thin shreds. Place these in a pan of cold water, bring slowly to the boil and cook for 5 minutes, then strain and refresh under cold water. Keep on one side.

Squeeze the juice from the lemon and orange and strain into a saucepan. Add the redcurrant jelly, heat gently and stir until dissolved, then boil for 5 minutes and add the port.

Blend the arrowroot with a little water then stir it carefully into the hot mixture. Cook, stirring, until the mixture thickens and clears. Stir in the Grand Marnier, if using.

Strain if necessary and add the shred of orange and lemon rind. Allow to cool so the sauce matures, then reheat to serve.

WILL NOT FREEZE, BUT WILL KEEP IN THE REFRIGERATOR FOR ABOUT A WEEK.

Chasseur or Huntsman's

This sauce is delicious with chicken, rabbit and veal, and may be added to the dish or served separately. It can be enriched with a little double cream.

MAKES 300 ML/½ PT

75 g/3 oz button mushrooms, sliced
25 g/1 oz butter
125 ml/4 fl oz white wine
2 tsp tomato purée
300 ml/½ pt espagnole sauce (see page 19)
2 tsp chopped mixed fresh herbs, e.g. parsley, marjoram and thyme

Cook the mushrooms lightly in half the butter, then add the wine and reduce by about half. Stir in the tomato purée and espagnole sauce and simmer for 2–3 minutes. Remove the pan from the heat and stir in the remaining butter and fresh herbs.

THIS WILL FREEZE VERY WELL.

Lyonnaise

A brown onion sauce to serve with grilled or roast meat.

MAKES 450 ML/¾ PT

25 g/1 oz butter
150 g/5 oz onion, chopped
125 ml/4 fl oz dry white wine
300 ml/½ pt espagnole sauce (see page 19)
1 tbsp white wine vinegar
Salt and pepper

Melt the butter in a pan, add the onion and cook until softened and lightly browned. Add the wine, increase the heat and cook until reduced by half. Stir in the sauce and cook for a further 10 minutes. Season and add the vinegar. Strain and purée the onion through a sieve or serve straight away.

SUITABLE FOR FREEZING.

Mornay

This is a cheese sauce with egg yolk and cream added at the end to enrich it. Serve over pasta, vegetables, eggs or fish, sprinkled with a little extra cheese and grilled to brown lightly.

MAKES ABOUT 450 ML/¾ PT

25 g/1 oz butter
25 g/1 oz plain flour
350 ml/12 fl oz milk, warmed
125 g/4 oz Gruyère cheese, finely grated
1 egg yolk
4 tbsp cream
½ tsp made mustard
Salt and pepper

Melt the butter in a pan, add the flour to make a roux and cook for 1 minute. Gradually add the milk as in basic white sauce (see page 17) and cook for 5 minutes.

Stir in the cheese and beat well to give a smooth consistency, then remove the pan from the heat.

Blend the egg yolk, cream and mustard together, stir in a little of the sauce then add this mixture to the pan and stir in carefully over a gentle heat, whisking if liked. If you let the sauce get too hot it will curdle. Season to taste.

NOT SUITABLE FOR FREEZING.

Robert

This is another demi-glace with piquant additions. Serve with pork or kidneys.

MAKES ABOUT 300 ML/½ PT

1 small onion, chopped
15 g/½ oz butter
3 tbsp red wine vinegar
300 ml/½ pt demi-glace (see page 19)
3 mini gherkins, chopped
2 tsp French mustard
2 tsp chopped fresh parsley

Cook the onion in the butter until softened, then add the vinegar and reduce by half. Add the demi-glace sauce and simmer for 10 minutes.

Just before serving, stir in the remaining ingredients.

DEMI-GLACE SAUCE IS SUITABLE FOR FREEZING; THAW AND FINISH THE SAUCE AS ABOVE.

Mustard

This is a basic white sauce flavoured with mustard and enriched with cream. Experiment with different types of mustard, and serve with pork or ham or over vegetables.

MAKES 300 ML/½ PT

300 ml/½ pt milk
Slice of onion
1 small bay leaf
Sprig of parsley
Salt and freshly ground white pepper
25 g/1 oz butter
1½ tbsp plain flour
2 tsp Dijon mustard
2 tsp horseradish sauce
4 tbsp double cream

Put the milk in a saucepan with the onion, bay leaf, parsley and a little salt and pepper. Slowly bring just to boiling point. Remove from the heat, allow to stand for 5 minutes then strain.

Using a clean pan, melt the butter, stir in the flour and cook for 1 minute. Gradually stir in the milk. Bring to the boil, stirring, and cook for 2 minutes.

Blend the mustard, horseradish and cream together and whisk carefully into the sauce.

THE BASIC SAUCE WILL FREEZE: THAW AND ADD THE CREAM AND MUSTARD WHEN REQUIRED.

Sweet and Hot Mustard

This could be served hot, stirred into strips of beef, chicken or pork. It is also good cold with hot sausages or frankfurters.

MAKES 450 ML/¾ PT

15 g/½ oz butter or margarine
1 small onion, finely chopped
25 g/1 oz granulated sugar
300 ml/½ pt dry white wine
150 ml/¼ pt white wine vinegar
25 g/1 oz cornflour
1 tsp dry mustard
1 tsp soy sauce
Salt and pepper (optional)

Melt the butter or margarine in a pan, add the onion and cook without browning, until soft, about 5 minutes. Remove the pan from the heat and stir in the sugar, wine and vinegar.

Blend the cornflour and mustard with a little water, stir into the sauce then bring slowly to the boil, stirring until the mixture thickens and clears. Reduce the heat and cook for 2 minutes. Stir in the soy sauce, taste and add seasoning if necessary.

SUITABLE FOR FREEZING.

Diable

This sauce should be served hot with grilled meat. It is usually prepared in small quantities.

MAKES 300 ML/½ PT

2 tbsp white wine
2 tbsp white wine vinegar
1 tbsp finely chopped shallots
300 ml/½ pt demi-glace (see page 19)
2 tsp tomato purée
Pinch of cayenne pepper
2 tsp Worcestershire sauce
A little chopped canned pimento (optional)
25 g/1 oz butter

Place the wine, vinegar and shallot in a small saucepan and cook gently to soften the shallot and reduce the liquid to 3 tbsp.

Stir in the demi-glace, tomato purée, a small pinch of cayenne and the Worcestershire sauce and cook for 2 minutes. Remove the pan from the heat and add the pimento, if using, and stir in the butter in small pieces.

THIS WILL FREEZE FOR A SHORT TIME ONLY, AS THE VINEGAR CHANGES ITS CHARACTER ON FREEZING.

Madeira

This can be made in two ways: either by reducing the Madeira with a little meat glaze and adding to a demi-glace, if available, or by starting from scratch. Serve with beef, tongue or calves' liver.

MAKES ABOUT 300 ML/½ PT

15 g/½ oz dripping or butter
2 tbsp finely chopped onion or shallot
1 rasher streaky bacon, finely chopped
1 tbsp plain flour
1 tsp tomato purée
125 ml/4 fl oz Madeira or sherry
A few mushroom stalks, chopped
Sprig of thyme
Sprig of parsley
450 ml/¾ pt good brown stock
Salt and pepper

Melt the fat in a pan, add the onion or shallot and bacon and cook slowly to brown without burning, otherwise the sauce will be bitter.

Stir in the flour and cook slowly to brown a little. Add the tomato purée and the Madeira or sherry and cook for a few minutes to reduce. Add the mushrooms and herbs then stir in the stock and a little seasoning. Bring to the boil and simmer for 15 minutes, allowing the sauce to reduce a little. Strain and return to pan to reheat and reduce more if necessary.

WILL FREEZE, BUT NOT FOR TOO LONG.

VARIATION

Périgueux

This is a Madeira sauce with chopped-up truffles and a little juice added – delicious but very expensive.

Although it would not be a traditional Périgueux, you can obtain quite a similar effect by rinsing and chopping up a few black olives or pickled walnuts, or even 2 or 3 prunes in an emergency.

Whipped Butter

This lightly whipped butter sauce may be flavoured with chopped fresh parsley, dill or tarragon. Crushed garlic mixed with parsley would make a good combination. Serve with vegetables or fish, or for spreading on warm bread or rolls.

MAKES 125 G/4 OZ

125 g/4 oz butter, at room temperature

Place the butter in a bowl and, using a tablespoon which should occasionally be dipped in warm water, cream the butter until light and fluffy. The butter will take up some of the water to lighten it.

Note: There are no short cuts to this but it does not take long and is worth the effort. Softening or slightly melting the butter does not give the best results.

NOT SUITABLE FOR FREEZING.

Crab

This is good served over halibut or similar firm white fish.

MAKES 750 ML/1¼ PT

600 ml/1 pt béchamel sauce (see page 17)
175 g/6 oz can white crabmeat
1–2 tbsp chopped fresh parsley

Make the sauce in the usual way. Drain the crabmeat well and check for any bones, then flake any pieces and add to the sauce with the parsley. Heat gently and serve.

THIS WOULD FREEZE, BUT IT IS BETTER TO FREEZE THE BASIC BECHAMEL AND ADD THE CRAB WHEN THAWED.

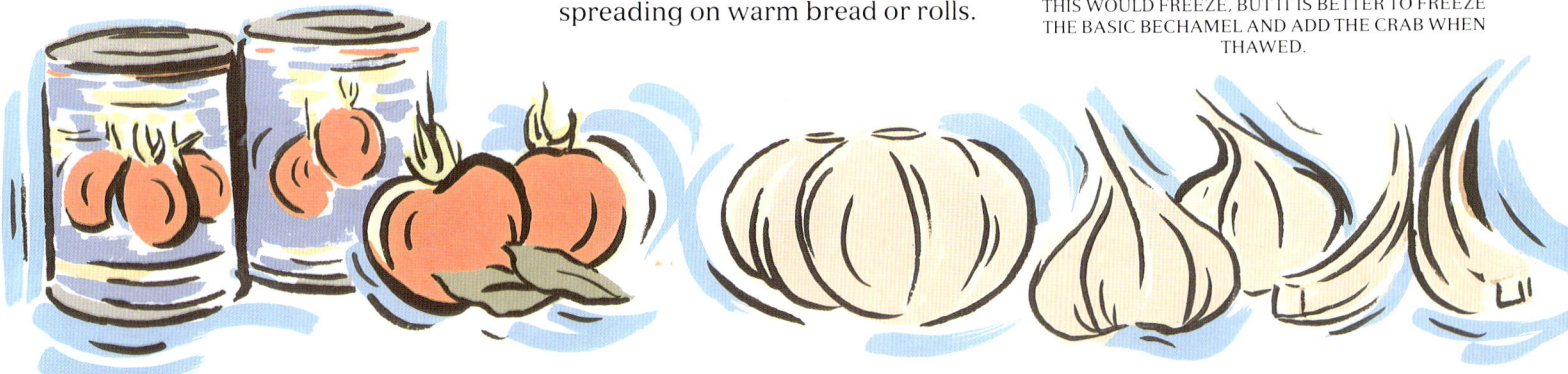

CHAPTER FIVE

Vegetable Sauces

~

Broccoli with Lemon

A simple, light vegetable sauce which would be good served with fish, chicken or other vegetables.

MAKES ABOUT 450 ML/¾ PT

225 g/8 oz fresh broccoli, washed
300 ml/½ pt vegetable stock
25 g/1 oz beurre manié (see page 7)
Juice of ½ lemon
2 tbsp double cream
Freshly ground pepper

Chop the broccoli stalks and cut the florets into small pieces. Cook these in the vegetable stock until just tender. Remove from the heat.

Using a slotted spoon, lift out a few of the florets. Whisk in the *beurre manié* in small pieces, then return the pan to the heat, making sure the *beurre manié* has dissolved. Bring to the boil, then cook for 2 minutes.

Return the reserved pieces of broccoli to the pan with the remaining ingredients.

THIS CAN BE FROZEN FOR A SHORT TIME WITH THE LEMON.

Carrot

This purée of carrots thickened with cream cheese is ideal to serve with other vegetables.

MAKES 600 ML/1 PT

325 g/12 oz carrots, sliced
450 ml/¾ pt vegetable stock
1 tbsp tarragon vinegar
Salt and freshly ground white pepper
50 g/2 oz low-fat cream cheese

Cook the carrots in the stock for about 10 minutes, until softened. Purée the carrots and the stock then blend in the remaining ingredients. Serve either hot or cold.

WILL FREEZE FOR AROUND A MONTH.

Cold Creole

Serve over eggs and vegetable dishes.

MAKES 300 ML/½ PT

225 g/8 oz tomato purée
3 tbsp fresh lime juice
125 g/4 oz onions, finely chopped
1 small stick celery, finely chopped
1 tsp finely chopped fresh chilli
1 tsp salt
4 stuffed olives, chopped
1 tbsp chopped fresh parsley (optional)

Mix all the ingredients together and serve.

SUITABLE FOR FREEZING.

Spinach

This is a delicious simple sauce. Serve over eggs, vegetables or pasta, or combine with eggs to make a flan filling. For a thinner sauce, add a little cream or milk.

MAKES 175 ML/6 FL OZ

175 g/6 oz spinach leaves
2 tbsp water
125 g/4 oz cream cheese
Salt and freshly ground pepper
Pinch of freshly grated nutmeg

Wash the spinach then put it in a small sauce with the water. Cook gently until wilted then sieve or purée in a food processor.

Return the spinach to the saucepan and stir in the cream cheese with seasoning and nutmeg to taste.

THIS WILL FREEZE FOR A SHORT TIME, OR YOU CAN FREEZE THE SPINACH PURÉE IN SMALL AMOUNTS THEN THAW AND ADD THE CREAM CHEESE AND SEASONING WHEN REQUIRED.

Cucumber and Dill

Try a different way with cucumber, excellent served with fish or vegetables.

MAKES 300 ML/½ PT

125 g/4 oz cucumber, peeled and cut into small dice
40 g/1½ oz butter
25 g/1 oz plain flour
300 ml/½ pt milk
1 egg yolk
2 tbsp single cream
1 tbsp chopped fresh dill
Salt and freshly ground white pepper

Sauté the cucumber in 15 g/½ oz of the butter until it is slightly softened but still retains some texture. Transfer to a plate.

Melt the remaining butter in the pan, add the flour and cook for 2 minutes then gradually stir in the milk. Bring to the boil, stirring, and cook for 3 minutes. Remove the pan from the heat.

Mix together the egg yolk and cream then beat this mixture into the sauce. Return the pan to the heat and cook for about 2 minutes, stirring, for the egg to cook and thicken.

Stir in the reserved cucumber with the dill, salt and pepper.

NOT SUITABLE FOR FREEZING.

Celeriac and Coriander

An unusual combination, suitable for serving with vegetables or fish. It could also be used as a base for soup.

MAKES ABOUT 450 ML/¾ PT

450 g/1 lb celeriac, peeled and diced
1 medium potato, peeled and sliced
450 ml/¾ pt water
1 tbsp ground coriander
150 ml/¼ pt Greek yogurt
Salt and pepper

Put the celeriac and potato in a saucepan with the water and coriander. Bring to the boil then cook for about 15 minutes until the vegetables are tender. Mash well or purée, then stir in the yogurt, salt and pepper.

THIS WILL FREEZE AS A PURÉE;
ADD THE YOGURT WHEN REQUIRED.

Garlic and Parsley

Although there is a lot of garlic in this sauce, the flavour is quite sweet and mild because the cloves are left whole. Use really fresh garlic. It's good with vegetables and pasta, and would also go well with chicken and fish.

MAKES ABOUT 300 ML/½ PT

14 even-sized cloves garlic, peeled
15 g/½ oz butter
200 ml/7 fl oz crème fraîche
40 g/1½ oz ground almonds
2 tbsp chopped fresh parsley
Salt and pepper

Place the garlic cloves and butter in a small frying pan and cook over a moderate heat until the garlic has lightly browned. Keep moving the cloves around so they don't brown too quickly.

Add the crème fraîche to the pan, stir until melted then stir in the remaining ingredients and heat through. Serve hot or cold or as a dip with extra cream or milk added to give the required consistency.

FREEZING IS NOT RECOMMENDED AS THE TEXTURE WOULD BE RUINED.

Peperoni

A mixture of peppers makes this a colourful sauce.

MAKES 450 ML/¾ PT

3 small peppers, red, green and yellow
3 tbsp olive oil
25 g/1 oz butter or margarine
1 large onion, sliced
1 carrot, peeled and cut into strips
3 tbsp plain flour
150 ml/¼ pt white wine
300 ml/½ pt stock
Salt and pepper

Wash and deseed the peppers then slice them fairly thinly. Heat the oil and the butter or margarine in a saucepan then add the onion, carrot and peppers. Cook until soft but not brown, about 8 minutes.

Stir in the flour and cook for 1 minute. Gradually stir in the wine and cook for a few seconds then stir in the stock. Bring to the boil, stirring gently so as not to break up the vegetables too much. Cook gently for about 4 minutes. Add seasoning to taste.

THIS WILL FREEZE WELL.

Ratatouille

This is quick to make as all the ingredients are cut up small to reduce the cooking time. A colourful and versatile sauce that could be used in many dishes: try it as a filling for flans, or an accompaniment to lamb, chicken, pork, eggs, pasta and vegetables.

MAKES 600 ML/1 PT

1 medium aubergine
1 medium courgette
½ small red pepper
5 tbsp olive oil
1 onion, chopped
1 clove garlic, crushed
400 g/14 oz can chopped tomatoes
2 tbsp chopped fresh parsley
Salt and pepper

Cut the aubergine into very small dice. Sprinkle with salt, and leave for 30 minutes. Drain, rinse and pat dry.

Heat 3 tbsp of the oil in a fairly large saucepan, add the aubergine and fry quite quickly until transparent. Remove and transfer to a colander placed over a bowl to drain.

Dice the courgette and pepper. Add the remaining oil to the saucepan and cook the onion and garlic for a few minutes, then add the pepper and courgettes and cook gently until these have softened a little. Return the aubergine to the pan with the tomatoes and cook, stirring gently, until the tomatoes have reduced a little but the vegetables still retain their shape.

Add the parsley, salt and pepper to taste, then serve at once.

THIS WILL FREEZE WELL.

Leek and Pepper

Serve with roast lamb, pasta or vegetables.

MAKES ABOUT 450 ML/¾ PT

225 g/8 oz leeks (weighed after trimming)
40 g/1½ oz butter or margarine
25 g/1 oz plain flour
450 ml/¾ pt milk
2 canned red pimentos
Salt and pepper

Cut the leeks into thin slices. Melt the butter or margarine in a pan, add the leeks, cover and cook without browning for 10 minutes, stirring occasionally.

Stir in the flour and cook gently for 3 minutes. Gradually add the milk, bring to the boil, stirring, and simmer for 2 minutes.

Drain the red pimentos well, cut into strips and add to the sauce. Heat through then season to taste.

SUITABLE FOR FREEZING.

Minted Pea Purée

This refreshing purée can be served over vegetables or with ham or eggs. It is also a good base for soup.

MAKES 300 ML/½ PT

15 g/½ oz butter
1 large spring onion, chopped
225 g/8 oz peas
150 ml/¼ pt vegetable stock
Sprig of thyme
2 tbsp crème fraîche
Salt and freshly ground pepper
1–2 tbsp chopped fresh mint

Melt the butter in a saucepan, add the spring onion and cook until softened. Add the peas.

Pour the stock over the peas with the leaves from the thyme. Cover and cook on a medium heat for about 10 minutes, until the peas are tender.

Liquidize or sieve the mixture then return it to the pan and add the crème fraîche, seasoning and mint. Heat through and serve.

WILL FREEZE PERFECTLY.

Red Peppercorn and Cream

A simple sauce to serve over fish.

MAKES 300 ML/½ PT

2 tsp red peppercorns
50 g/2 oz unsalted butter
300 ml/½ pt double cream
Salt
1 tbsp chopped fresh parsley

Crush the peppercorns. Melt the butter in a small frying pan over a low heat, then add the peppercorns. Cook very briefly to extract a little of the flavour.

Quickly add the cream, increase the heat and stir very thoroughly so the ingredients blend together. Add a little salt.

Pour into a warmed sauceboat, sprinkle with the chopped parsley and serve at once.

NOT SUITABLE FOR FREEZING.

Tarragon and Parsley

Try this sauce with courgettes, marrow or whole new carrots, leeks and broad beans. It's also good with chicken and poached fish.

MAKES 300 ML/½ PT

40 g/1½ oz butter or margarine
3 tbsp plain flour
300 ml/½ pt milk, or half milk and half stock
1 tbsp chopped fresh tarragon
2 tbsp chopped fresh parsley
2 tbsp cream
Salt and freshly ground white pepper

Melt the butter or margarine in a pan, add the flour and cook without browning for 2 minutes.

Gradually add the liquid off the heat, then return the pan to the heat and bring to the boil, stirring. Reduce the heat and cook for about 5 minutes.

Remove the pan from the heat and add the remaining ingredients. Do not allow the sauce to boil again.

THIS WILL FREEZE, BUT REHEAT IT VERY SLOWLY BECAUSE OF THE CREAM.

Sweetcorn

This sweet-tasting sauce is sharpened by the addition of lemon juice. Serve it over vegetables, as part of a bean dish, or with chicken or bacon.

MAKES ABOUT 600 ML/1 PT

1 small leek, trimmed
1 stick celery, chopped
25 g/1 oz butter or margarine
2 rashers streaky bacon, chopped (optional)
425 g/15 oz can creamed sweetcorn
1 tomato, deseeded and chopped
1 tbsp lemon juice
Salt and freshly ground pepper

Put the leek and celery in a saucepan with the butter or margarine and cook slowly to soften the vegetables. Add the bacon halfway through, if using.

When the vegetables are soft add the remaining ingredients and heat through.

THIS SAUCE IS SO QUICK TO MAKE, IT'S NOT NECESSARY TO FREEZE IT.

Celery

This is very good served over artichokes, or you can add cooked chestnuts and serve with Brussels sprouts. Delicious poured over nut roast.

MAKES 450 ML/¾ PT

450 ml/¾ pt milk
3 sticks celery, washed and thinly sliced
75 g/3 oz butter
3 tbsp plain flour
Nutmeg (optional)

Pour the milk into a pan, add the celery and cook slowly, covered, until tender, about 15 minutes. Strain the milk and reserve the celery.

Melt half the butter in a pan, stir in the flour and cook for 1 minute. Remove the pan from the heat and gradually stir in the milk. Return to the heat then bring to the boil, stirring, and cook for 3 minutes. Stir in the celery and remaining butter and nutmeg if liked. Do not allow the sauce to boil.

SUITABLE FOR FREEZING. REHEAT BY ADDING A LITTLE MILK.

Curried Parsnip and Celery

This delicately flavoured vegetable purée could easily be made into a soup by adding milk. Serve over cauliflower, carrots or eggs.

MAKES 450 ML/¾ PT

2 tbsp oil
1 small onion, chopped
2 tsp ground cumin
1 tsp ground coriander
1 stick celery, sliced
225 g/8 oz parsnips, peeled and diced
450 ml/¾ pt water
1 tsp salt

Heat the oil in a pan, add the onion and cook until softened. Stir in the cumin and coriander and cook for 30 seconds, stirring.

Add all the remaining ingredients, bring to the boil, stirring, then reduce the heat and simmer for 20 minutes. When the vegetables are tender, sieve or liquidize the sauce.

SUITABLE FOR FREEZING.

Romaine

This sauce goes with vegetable dishes or over beef, lamb, chicken or fish.

MAKES 300 ML/½ PT

40 g/1½ oz butter or margarine
1 medium onion, chopped
1 small turnip, finely diced
2 small carrots, thinly sliced
1 stick celery, thinly sliced
½–1 tsp dried mixed herbs, to taste
2 tbsp plain flour
1 tbsp dry sherry
300 ml/½ pt vegetable stock
1 tbsp chopped fresh parsley
Salt and pepper

Melt the butter or margarine in a pan, add the onion and cook gently for 5 minutes. Add the turnip, carrots, celery and herbs, stir around then cover with a piece of damp greaseproof paper. Put the lid on the pan and cook gently for 10 minutes, until the vegetables are just tender.

Stir in the flour and cook for 1 minute, then add the sherry. Gradually stir in the stock, bring to the boil and cook for 2 minutes. Add the parsley and seasoning to taste.

THIS WILL FREEZE WELL.

Tomato and Marjoram

This is a short-cut sauce using canned tomatoes. It makes a good basis for pasta sauces, and it can also be turned into a barbecue sauce.

MAKES 300 ML/½ PT

2 tbsp olive oil
1 onion, chopped
1 small green pepper, deseeded and diced
2 cloves garlic, crushed
400 g/14 oz can peeled tomatoes
1 tbsp tomato purée
1 tbsp demerara sugar
2 tsp dried marjoram
Salt and pepper

Extras for a quick barbecue sauce:
2 tbsp sweet pickle
1 tsp Worcestershire sauce
½ tsp made mustard
2 tsp cider vinegar

Place the oil in a saucepan, add the onion and cook for 5 minutes without browning. Stir in the green pepper, garlic and tomatoes.

Cover and simmer for 15 minutes, then stir in the tomato purée, sugar, marjoram and salt and pepper. Continue cooking, without the lid, for a further 10–15 minutes, until the sauce has reduced. Taste and adjust the seasoning.

To make a quick barbecue sauce, add the extra ingredients at the same time as the sugar, etc.

This sauce will keep well for a few days, and can be served hot or cold.

IT WILL ALSO FREEZE WELL.

Red Wine and Paprika

This is an unusual sauce to serve over artichokes, cauliflower, beef or lamb steaks or pork.

MAKES ABOUT 450 ML/¾ PT

40 g/1½ oz butter or margarine
1 small red pepper, deseeded and thinly sliced
2 tsp paprika pepper
3 tbsp plain flour
2 tbsp red wine
300 ml/½ pt milk
150 ml/¼ pt vegetable stock
Salt and freshly ground pepper

Melt the butter or margarine in a pan, stir in the red pepper and cook until just softened, about 3 minutes. Stir in the paprika and flour and cook for 2 minutes then pour in the wine.

Gradually add the milk and stock then bring to the boil, stirring, and simmer for about 6 minutes to reduce the sauce and allow the flavours to develop. Taste and adjust the seasoning.

FREEZE IN RIGID CONTAINERS.

Tomato and Lentil

Serve over eggs, vegetables or rice.

MAKES 450 ML/¾ PT

2 tbsp oil
1 small onion, chopped
1 stick celery, chopped
1 carrot, cut into small dice
1 small parsnip, cut into small dice
1 tsp ground cumin
1 tbsp tomato purée
50 g/2 oz green lentils, washed
450 ml/¾ pt vegetable stock, or water and 1 vegetable stock cube
Sprig of parsley
Salt and freshly ground pepper
1 tsp cornflour (optional)

Heat the oil in a pan and lightly sauté the onion, celery, carrot and parsnip for 5 minutes just to soften.

Add the cumin, stir and cook for 30 seconds, then add the tomato purée, lentils, stock, parsley and a little pepper. Cover and cook gently for 20–25 minutes, stirring occasionally to ensure the lentils cook evenly. For a thicker sauce, blend the cornflour with a little water, add a little of the hot mixture to it, then stir it into the pan and cook for 3 minutes. Taste, and season if necessary.

THIS SAUCE FREEZES WELL.

Mushroom and Sherry

There are three ways of making this sauce; the mushrooms can be cooked in butter and added to a white sauce; for a rich, dark sauce, they can be finely chopped and cooked with finely chopped onion and parsley then added to a white sauce; or they can be cooked as part of the sauce, as in the recipe below. A little sherry and cream could also be added.

MAKES 450 ML/¾ PT

50 g/2 oz butter
1 spring onion, thinly sliced (optional)
125 g/4 oz button mushrooms, wiped and sliced
40 g/1½ oz plain flour
2 tbsp dry sherry
300 ml/½ pt warm milk
Salt and freshly ground white pepper

Melt the butter in a pan, add the spring onion, if using, and the mushrooms and cook until softened.

Stir in the flour, add the sherry, gradually add the milk, then bring to the boil, stirring, and cook for 5 minutes. Season to taste.

FREEZES VERY WELL.

Tomato and Mozzarella

This sauce is made with passata, a commercial tomato purée easily available in most supermarkets. Serve with pasta, pork, chicken or vegetables.

MAKES 450 ML/¾ PT

2 tbsp oil
1 large onion, chopped
1 clove garlic, crushed
1 bay leaf
500 ml/16 fl oz carton passata
125 g/4 oz mozzarella cheese, diced
8 olives, sliced
a few fresh basil leaves, shredded

Heat the oil in a pan, add the onion, garlic and bay leaf and cook gently, covered, for 15 minutes.

Stir in the passata and cook for a further 15 minutes, then remove the pan from the heat and stir in the remaining ingredients.

A QUICK SAUCE TO MAKE, SO NOT WORTH FREEZING AND TAKING UP SPACE.

CHAPTER SIX

Pasta Sauces

~

Leek and Bacon

These ingredients are always handy to have in stock as they are so versatile – use in pasta sauces, quiches and omelettes or with rice. This sauce is an ideal consistency for pasta, it will need 50 ml/2 fl oz more stock if a pouring sauce is required.

SERVES 3–4

1 medium leek, trimmed and thinly sliced
4 rashers streaky bacon, chopped
50 g/2 oz mushrooms, sliced
2 tbsp plain flour
225 ml/8 fl oz chicken stock
3 tbsp cream
1 tbsp chopped fresh parsley
Freshly ground pepper

Melt a knob of butter in a pan, stir in the leek and bacon and cook gently, stirring occasionally, for about 5 minutes to soften the leek.

Stir in the mushrooms, cook for 1 minute then add the flour and cook for 2 minutes. Gradually stir in the chicken stock, bring to the boil, stirring, and cook for 5 minutes.

Add the remaining ingredients, stir around and heat through. Serve with pasta or over chicken joints.

SUITABLE FOR FREEZING BUT LEAVE OUT THE CREAM.

Bacon, Blue Cheese and Celery

These ingredients make an interesting sauce which can be used with vegetables or stirred into pasta.

SERVES 4–5

3 sticks celery, washed and sliced
450 ml/¾ pt milk
40 g/1½ oz butter or margarine
3 rashers streaky bacon, chopped
3 tbsp plain flour
75 g/3 oz Danish blue cheese, cubed
Freshly ground pepper

Place the celery in a saucepan with the milk, cover and simmer gently for 12–15 minutes until the celery is tender. Strain the milk, reserving the celery.

Melt the butter or margarine in a pan, add the bacon for 2 minutes. Add the flour, and cook for 2 minutes, stirring all the time. Remove the pan from the heat and gradually add the strained milk. Return the pan to the heat and cook, stirring, until the sauce thickens, about 3–5 minutes.

Add the reserved celery, the cheese, and pepper to taste. Heat through to melt the cheese.

FREEZE FOR ABOUT 1–2 MONTHS ONLY, BECAUSE OF THE BACON.

Seafood

Shelled prawns and mussels are now available in cans or cooked and chilled. The fish may be varied according to availability. For a really luxurious sauce, make the richer version of velouté (see page 20).

SERVES 3–4

350 g/12 oz mixed fresh fish, e.g. monkfish, squid, scallops
450 ml/¾ pt water
Velouté sauce (whole quantity – see page 20), made with the liquid from cooking the fish (see method)
125 g/4 oz peeled prawns
125 g/4 oz cooked mussels

Prepare the fish: cut into cubes or rings and poach in the water, adding the squid first as it takes longer. Cook until just tender. Remove the fish with a slotted spoon and reserve the liquor.

Make the velouté sauce, using the fish liquor, then stir in the cooked fish and shellfish. Serve with pasta.

NOT SUITABLE FOR FREEZING; HAVE THE SAUCE IN THE FREEZER AND ADD THE FISH WHEN REQUIRED.

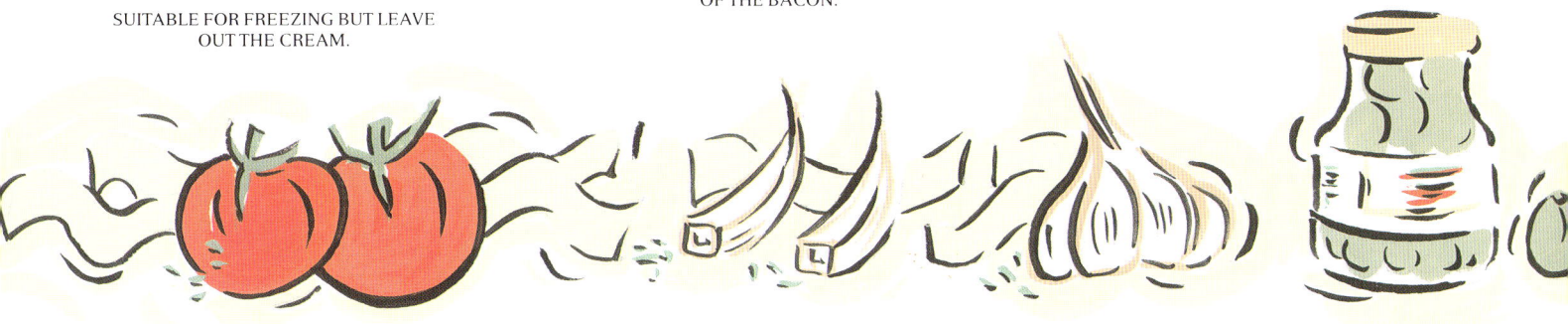

Chicken Liver

A cheap, flavoursome sauce. The herbs may be left out if unavailable.

SERVES 4

3 tbsp olive oil
50 g/2 oz streaky bacon, chopped
1 small onion, finely chopped
1 clove garlic, crushed
225 g/8 oz chicken livers, trimmed and finely chopped
50 g/2 oz mushrooms, finely chopped
1 tbsp plain flour
2 tbsp medium sherry, Marsala or Martini
1 tbsp tomato purée
300 ml/½ pt chicken stock
1 tbsp chopped fresh marjoram or oregano (optional)
Salt and pepper

Place the oil, bacon, onion and garlic in a saucepan and cook slowly for about 10 minutes to soften the onion.

Stir in the chicken livers, mushrooms and cook until they change colour, 2–3 minutes. Add the flour, cook for a further minute, then add the wine, allow it to bubble, and stir in the tomato purée. Gradually add the stock, stirring, then add the herbs, if using, and salt and pepper.

Cover and simmer gently for about 30 minutes. Serve with pasta or rice.

SUITABLE FOR FREEZING.

Chilli Beef

The amount of chilli powder you add depends on how hot you like your food. Use a mild chilli powder, if preferred. If you like, serve yoghurt with this sauce.

SERVES 3–4

1 tbsp oil
225 g/8 oz lean minced beef
1 onion, chopped
1 stick celery, chopped
2 cloves garlic, crushed
1–2 tsp hot chilli powder
2 tbsp tomato purée
1 tbsp plain flour
225 g/8 oz can chopped tomatoes
150 ml/¼ pt water

Heat the oil in a pan, add the mince and sauté until the meat is no longer red. Add the onion, celery and garlic and cook until the vegetables are soft, about 8 minutes.

Stir in the remaining ingredients and cook for 30 minutes.

THIS FREEZES WELL; MAKE DOUBLE AND FREEZE IN SMALL CONTAINERS.

Bolognaise

There are many versions of this type of sauce and not all of them include wine, but the addition of alcohol does make it a bit special. If you prefer to leave it out, increase the amount of stock. Serve with pasta, rice or chicken.

SERVES 3–4

1 tbsp olive oil
1 onion, chopped
175 g/6 oz lean minced beef
50 g/2 oz chicken livers, washed and chopped
125 g/4 oz mushrooms, chopped
1 tbsp plain flour
300 ml/½ pt beef stock
1 clove garlic, crushed
1 bay leaf
150 ml/¼ pt red wine or sherry
3 tbsp tomato purée
Salt and pepper

Put the oil in a saucepan, add the onion and fry until lightly browned. Stir in all the meat and cook briskly to lose the bright colour. Add the mushrooms.

Sprinkle in the flour and stir around, then gradually add the stock and bring to a simmer. Add the remaining ingredients and the tomato purée and seasoning to taste and bring back to a simmer. Cover and cook gently, stirring occasionally, for about 45 minutes.

IT IS ALWAYS USEFUL TO HAVE THIS SAUCE IN THE FREEZER, AND WORTH MAKING IN BULK.

Tomato and Olive

This uses fresh tomatoes, but canned tomatoes can be substituted if necessary.

MAKES 450 ML/¾ PT

1 tbsp olive oil
1 onion, chopped
1 clove garlic, crushed
450 g/1 lb fresh tomatoes, skinned and chopped
2 tbsp wine or cider vinegar
1 tsp Worcestershire sauce
75 g/3 oz stuffed olives, chopped
25 g/1 oz black olives, stoned and chopped
2 tbsp chopped fresh parsley, or
1 tbsp chopped fresh basil

Heat the oil in a saucepan, add the onion and cook without browning until soft, about 2 minutes.

Stir in the garlic and tomatoes and cook down to a pulp, about 10 minutes.

Add the remaining ingredients. Heat through and serve with pasta, and with Parmesan cheese, if liked.

SUITABLE FOR FREEZING.

Spanish

SERVES 3–4

3 tbsp olive oil
2 Spanish onions, thinly sliced
225 g/8 oz button mushrooms, sliced
2 cloves garlic, crushed
50 g/2 oz can anchovies, well drained
10 pimento-stuffed olives, halved
3 tbsp cream
Freshly ground pepper
2 tbsp chopped fresh parsley
Freshly grated Parmesan cheese

Heat the oil in a pan and cook the onions until just softened. Stir in the mushrooms, garlic, anchovies, olives, cream, pepper and parsley. Heat through and serve over pasta, sprinkled with Parmesan cheese.

NOT SUITABLE FOR FREEZING.

Vegetarian Pasta

MAKES ABOUT 300 ML/½ PT

2 tsp olive oil
50 g/2 oz red pepper, finely sliced
2 leaves spinach, washed and finely chopped
1 clove garlic, crushed
2 tsp chopped fresh sage
40 g/1½ oz walnuts, chopped
200 ml/7 fl oz fromage frais
1 tsp cornflour
1 tsp freshly grated Parmesan cheese
Freshly ground pepper

Put the oil in a saucepan with the red pepper and spinach. Cook gently to soften the vegetables, about 5 minutes, then stir in the garlic, sage and walnuts and cook for 30 seconds.

Blend the cornflour with the fromage frais and stir into the vegetables. Cook for 1 minute to thicken slightly then add the Parmesan and pepper.

NOT SUITABLE FOR FREEZING.

CHAPTER SEVEN

Sauces from Around the World

~

Creole

This sauce is suitable to serve with sausages, omelettes and some vegetables.

MAKES 600 ML/1 PT

1 red pepper
1 green pepper
2 tbsp olive oil
2 onions, chopped
1 clove garlic, crushed (optional)
400 g/14 oz can chopped tomatoes
Salt and freshly ground pepper
1 tbsp cornflour
1 tsp caster sugar, or to taste

Deseed the peppers and slice fairly thinly. Put the oil in a saucepan with the peppers and onions. Cover and cook gently for about 10 minutes to soften.

Stir in the garlic, if using, with the tomatoes and seasoning. Bring to the boil and cook for about 10 minutes.

Blend the cornflour with a little water and stir into the pan. Bring to the boil, stirring, and cook until thickened. Stir in the sugar and adjust the seasoning to taste.

THIS FREEZES WELL.

Mexican Green Salsa

This sauce is hot because of the chillies. Taking out the seeds gives a gentler heat. Serve with chicken, spicy sausages or filled tortillas.

MAKES 300 ML/½ PT

350 g/12 oz green tomatoes, chopped
50 g/2 oz onion, chopped
2 cloves garlic, crushed
2 tbsp finely chopped fresh parsley
2 small green chillies, sliced
Salt and pepper

Place all the ingredients in a saucepan and bring slowly to the boil. Simmer gently until the tomatoes are soft. Using a potato masher, break down the sauce and adjust the seasoning if necessary.

WILL FREEZE.

Bagna Cauda

This is a traditional Italian sauce to serve with raw vegetables or crisp bread or grissini sticks. It's truly wonderful with globe artichokes.

MAKES ABOUT 150 ML/¼ PT

50 g/2 oz can anchovies in olive oil
75 g/3 oz unsalted butter
6 cloves garlic, crushed
2 tbsp olive oil

Using a pair of kitchen scissors, snip the anchovies into small pieces in the can.

Melt the butter in a pan and add all the ingredients, including the anchovies and their oil. Cover and cook very gently for 10 minutes. Serve hot, straight away.

NOT SUITABLE FOR FREEZING.

Raita

This Indian relish is served with spicy food to cool it down. A refreshing dish which goes well with samosas, curries and barbecued food.

MAKES 600 ML/1 PT

12 cm/5 in piece of cucumber
Salt and pepper
600 ml/1 pt plain yogurt
2–3 tbsp chopped fresh mint
Garam masala and paprika

Peel and coarsely grate the cucumber then place it in a nylon sieve over a bowl and sprinkle with a little salt. Leave for 15 minutes then press out most of the juice.

Put the yogurt in a bowl, stir with a fork then add the cucumber, mint and seasoning. Serve sprinkled with garam masala and paprika.

NOT SUITABLE FOR FREEZING.

Sweet and Sour

A versatile sauce derived from Chinese cookery but now served with chicken, duck, turkey and crispy battered and crumbed products.

MAKES 450 ML/¾ PT

2 tbsp oil
1 small carrot, cut into shreds
1 small leek, trimmed and thinly sliced
½ small red pepper
1 large clove garlic, crushed
300 ml/½ pt chicken stock
1 tbsp cornflour
1 tbsp soy sauce
1–2 tbsp white wine vinegar
1 tsp sugar
Salt and pepper

Heat the oil in a pan, add the vegetables and cook, stirring, for about 5 minutes. Do not let the vegetables brown.

Stir in the garlic, add the chicken stock and cook for a further 5 minutes. Blend the cornflour, soy sauce and vinegar adding a little of the hot stock as well, then pour into the pan and cook for 3 minutes or until the sauce has thickened. Stir in the sugar, salt and pepper to taste.

SUITABLE FOR FREEZING.

Black Bean

A traditional Chinese sauce authentically served with steamed fish or chicken. It may also be served with grilled or poached fish or poultry, or used as the cooking medium for finely sliced beef steak, pork or lamb after a brief stir-frying.

MAKES 150 ML/¼ PT

1 tsp sesame oil
1 tbsp oil
25 g/1 oz fresh ginger root, peeled and cut into fine strips
4 large spring onions, finely shredded diagonally
1 large clove garlic, finely chopped
150 ml/¼ pt dry sherry
3 tbsp salted black beans
1 tbsp lemon juice
2 tbsp soy sauce
1 tsp sugar
1 tsp cornflour (optional)

Heat the oils in a wok, add the ginger, spring onions and garlic and cook for about 3 minutes. Stir in the remaining ingredients and cook, covered, for 15 minutes.

If liked, thicken slightly by blending the cornflour with 2 tbsp water then stirring it into the sauce. Bring to the boil, stirring, and simmer for 2 minutes.

MAKE AND USE THE SAME DAY.

Teriyaki

This Japanese sauce is used both as a marinade and as a coating for grilled foods such as chicken, beef and pork. It may also be brushed over skewered foods such as chicken and spring onions before grilling, or served as a coating sauce.

MAKES ABOUT 450 ML/¾ PT

2 tbsp spring onions, finely chopped
3 cloves garlic, crushed
1 tbsp grated fresh ginger root
1 tsp sesame oil
200 ml/7 fl oz Japanese soy sauce
100 ml/4 fl oz Japanese saki or dry sherry
3 tbsp sugar
175 ml/6 fl oz chicken stock
1 tsp cornflour

Place the spring onions, garlic and ginger in a saucepan with the sesame oil and cook slowly for a few seconds. Add the soy sauce, saki or sherry, sugar and chicken stock. Bring to the boil and simmer for 10 minutes.

Blend the cornflour with a little water, add some of the hot liquid then return to the pan. Bring to the boil, stirring, then reduce the heat until the sauce thickens, about 2–3 minutes.

NOT SUITABLE FOR FREEZING.

Korma

Usually the meat is cooked in this popular Indian sauce. You could make the sauce in advance then add strips of sautéed chicken, allowing time for the flavours to mingle.

MAKES ABOUT 450 ML/¾ PT

3 tbsp oil
200 g/7 oz onion, finely chopped
25 g/1 oz ground almonds
½ tsp ground turmeric
1 tbsp ground cumin
2 tbsp ground coriander
2 tsp grated fresh ginger root
4 cloves garlic, crushed
300 ml/½ pt water
150 ml/¼ pt single cream
2 tsp salt

Heat the oil in a pan and slowly fry the onion until softened but not browned. Add the spices, ginger, garlic and ground almonds. Cook for 1 minute, then gradually add the water. Stir in the cream and salt and cook, covered, for about 30 minutes, stirring occasionally. The sauce should be fairly thick and creamy; if not, increase the heat to reduce it a little.

THIS WILL FREEZE WELL.

Coconut and Chilli

A modern sauce to serve hot over chicken or vegetables or to use as a side sauce for a vegetable curry or samosas.

MAKES 300 ML/½ PT

2 tbsp oil
1 onion, finely chopped
1 tsp grated fresh ginger root
1 green chilli, deseeded and finely chopped
2 cloves garlic, crushed
4 tsp curry powder
1 tsp turmeric
50 g/2 oz creamed coconut
450 ml/¾ pt hot water
Juice of 1 lime
2 tbsp cream

Heat the oil in a pan, add the onion and sauté without browning for about 5 minutes. Stir in the ginger, chilli and garlic and cook for 1 minute. Stir in the curry powder and turmeric and cook for 30 seconds. Remove the pan from the heat.

Dissolve the creamed coconut in the hot water then pour it into the pan and stir around. Bring the sauce to the boil, then reduce the heat, cover and simmer, stirring occasionally, for about 30 minutes or until the sauce has reduced and has thickened. Stir in the lime juice and cream.

THIS WILL FREEZE VERY WELL.

Pesto

This traditional Italian sauce for pasta freezes well and is a good way of using up fresh basil. Pecorino romano cheese could be used instead of Parmesan, and I have even used Gouda occasionally.

MAKES 150 ML/¼ PT

100 ml/4 fl oz virgin olive oil
50 g/2 oz fresh basil leaves
2 cloves garlic, crushed
2 tbsp pine nuts
Pinch of salt
Freshly ground black pepper
50 g/2 oz Parmesan cheese, freshly grated
2 tbsp cream (optional)

A food processor or blender can be used for this recipe, or use a pestle and mortar and blend the ingredients and oil gradually.

Place the oil, basil, garlic, pine nuts, salt and pepper in the food processor or blender and process until creamy. Transfer to a bowl and fold in the cheese and the cream, if using.

FREEZE IN SMALL AMOUNTS.

Barbecue

There are many variations of barbecue sauce and this is mine.

MAKES ABOUT 450 ML/¾ PT

25 g/1 oz butter
1 small onion, finely chopped
1 stick celery, finely chopped
1 clove garlic, crushed
2 tbsp dry mustard
2 tbsp demerara sugar
½ tsp Tabasco sauce
400 g/14 oz can tomato juice
2 tbsp Worcestershire sauce
Juice of 1 orange
4 tbsp wine vinegar
1 bay leaf
Salt and pepper

Melt the butter in a saucepan, add the onion and celery and cook for about 5 minutes until softened but not browned. Stir in the garlic and cook for 2 minutes.

Add the remaining ingredients, bring to the boil and simmer for 10–15 minutes. Adjust the seasoning and remove the bay leaf before serving either hot or cold.

IDEAL FOR FREEZING.

Gado-Gado

This is an Indonesian recipe which I have simplified by using crunchy peanut butter. If preferred, grind salted peanuts and adjust the consistency accordingly. Serve over mixed salads or vegetable dishes such as vegetable bakes, and with more water if required.

MAKES 300 ML/½ PT

2 tbsp oil
1 onion, finely chopped
1 tsp chilli powder
2 tsp fresh grated ginger root
1 clove garlic, crushed
175 g/6 oz crunchy peanut butter
300 ml/½ pt water
1 tbsp molasses
1 tbsp lemon juice
1 tsp soy sauce
2 tbsp single cream (optional)

Heat the oil in a pan, add the onion and cook for 3 minutes. Add the chilli, ginger and garlic and cook for 2 minutes, then allow to cool slightly.

Stir in all the remaining ingredients except the cream. The sauce will thicken as it cools; if necessary add extra water for a thinner sauce and the cream for a creamier sauce.

THIS WILL FREEZE FOR A SHORT TIME BUT MAY NEED THINNING AGAIN.

Satay

A simple Indonesian peanut sauce to serve with grilled skewered meats or fish.

MAKES 300 ML/½ PT

1 tbsp oil
1 small onion, finely chopped
1 tsp chilli powder
125 g/4 oz peanut butter
2 tsp soy sauce
1 tsp soft brown sugar
1 tbsp lemon juice
25 g/1 oz creamed coconut
150 ml/¼ pt hot water

Heat the oil in a pan and cook the onion until softened. Add the chilli powder and cook for 30 seconds, then stir in the peanut butter, soy sauce, sugar and lemon juice. Remove the pan from the heat.

Dissolve the coconut in the hot water and stir into the pan. Allow to cool before serving.

THIS WILL FREEZE FOR A SHORT TIME.

CHAPTER EIGHT

Savoury Fruit Sauces

~

Apple

This sauce may be served with pork, duck or goose.

MAKES 300 ML/½ PT

450 g/1 lb cooking apples
2–3 tbsp water
15 g/½ oz butter
Salt and pepper
2 tsp sugar (optional)

Peel, core and slice the apples then put them in a saucepan with the water. Cook gently to soften the apples for about 10 minutes. Stir in the remaining ingredients, adding sufficient sugar to take the sharpness away. Sieve for a smoother sauce, if liked.

THIS FREEZES VERY WELL AND IS WORTH MAKING IN LARGE QUANTITIES THEN DIVIDING BETWEEN SMALL FREEZER CONTAINERS.

Apple and Sloe

An unusual tangy combination.

MAKES ABOUT 300 ML/½ PT

125 g/4 oz ripe sloes
15 g/½ oz butter
1 small onion, chopped
5 tbsp water
225 g/8 oz cooking apples
3 juniper berries, crushed
Pinch of allspice (optional) and extra butter

Wash the sloes and remove the stalks. Melt the butter in a pan and cook the onion until soft, about 5 minutes. Stir in the sloes and water and cook until softened, about 5 minutes.

Peel, core and slice the apples and add them and the berries to the pan. Cook slowly until all the fruit is tender, adding a little water if necessary to prevent the sauce sticking. Stir in the allspice, if liked, and the extra butter.

SUITABLE FOR FREEZING.

Cherry Brandy

This sauce improves if kept for a day or two for the flavour to mature. Serve with duck or venison.

MAKES 600 ML/1 PT

1 tsp oil
1 small onion, finely chopped
3 tbsp port
3 tbsp cherry brandy
450 ml/¾ pt chicken stock
2 tbsp cornflour
Finely grated rind and juice of 1 orange
2 tbsp red wine vinegar
225 g/8 oz fresh or frozen cherries, pitted and halved

Heat the oil in a pan, add the onion and cook gently until softened, about 3 minutes. Stir in the port and cherry brandy and cook for 1 minute. Stir in most of the chicken stock then remove the pan from the heat.

Blend the cornflour with the remaining stock then stir it into the pan with the orange rind and juice. Bring slowly to the boil, stirring, then reduce the heat and simmer until thickened and clear, 3–5 minutes.

Stir in the wine vinegar and cherries and heat gently to warm the cherries. Serve the sauce hot or cold.

SUITABLE FOR FREEZING.

Orange

This is a good sauce to go with duck, pork, game and tongue. The addition of an orange liqueur gives it a lift.

MAKES 300 ML/½ PT

300 ml/½ pt espagnole sauce (see page 19)
300 ml/½ pt good brown stock
Juice and finely grated rind of 1 orange
1 tsp lemon juice
2 tbsp Grand Marnier
2 tbsp redcurrant jelly
Salt and freshly ground pepper

Pour the sauce and stock into a saucepan with the orange juice. Cook until reduced by half.

Meanwhile cook the grated orange rind in a small pan of cold water for 5 minutes to soften; drain well.

Strain the sauce and add the remaining ingredients, including the orange rind. Stir well to dissolve the redcurrant jelly. Taste and adjust the seasoning.

THIS WILL FREEZE WELL.

Redcurrant and Cider

Try this redcurrant sauce instead of gravy with turkey or lamb. Frozen redcurrants work very well instead of fresh.

MAKES ABOUT 600 ML/1 PT

25 g/1 oz onion, finely chopped
225 g/8 oz redcurrants
450 ml/¾ pt medium-sweet cider
150 ml/¼ pt red wine vinegar
25 g/1 oz caster sugar
1 tsp ready-made mustard
1 tbsp cornflour
Salt and pepper (optional)

Place the onion, redcurrants, cider, vinegar and sugar in a saucepan. Cook gently for 10 minutes until the onion and fruit are soft, then remove the pan from the heat.

Blend the mustard and cornflour with a little water, stir in some of the liquid from the pan, then return this mixture to the pan, stirring it in carefully. Bring to the boil, stirring and cook for 3–5 minutes until the mixture thickens and clears.

Add seasoning if necessary and extra sugar if required.

SUITABLE FOR FREEZING.

Savoury Marmalade

This sauce is convenient to make as it uses store-cupboard ingredients. Serve hot with pork chops or gammon steaks. Orange and ginger marmalade would be an interesting variation.

MAKES ABOUT 150 ML/¼ PT

40 g/1½ oz butter or margarine
1 onion, thinly sliced
6 tbsp orange marmalade
2 tbsp white wine vinegar
2 tbsp soft brown sugar, or to taste
Salt and pepper

Melt the butter or margarine in a saucepan, add the onion and cook gently without browning until soft. Stir in the marmalade and vinegar, adding sugar, salt and pepper to taste.

SUITABLE FOR FREEZING.

Apricot Curry

A simple, fruity curry sauce to go with chicken, lamb, pork and vegetables.

MAKES ABOUT 300 ML/½ PT

125 g/4 oz dried apricots
2 tbsp oil
1 medium onion, coarsely chopped
1½ tbsp curry powder
2 tbsp plain flour
450 ml/¾ pt water
1 tsp tomato purée
½ tsp salt

Cover the apricots with boiling water while preparing the sauce.

Heat the oil in a pan and cook the onion for 5 minutes without browning. Stir in the curry powder and cook gently for 2 minutes. Stir in the flour and cook for 1 minute. Gradually add the water then bring to the boil, stirring. Cook for 2 minutes.

Drain and chop the apricots, add them to the sauce then cover and simmer gently for 20 minutes. Add the tomato purée and salt.

THIS WILL FREEZE WELL.

Gooseberry

Traditionally this sauce is served with mackerel, but it may also be served with pork and gammon steaks or bacon joints. For a thicker sauce, add 25 g/1 oz *beurre manié* (see page 7).

MAKES 300 ML/½ PT

225 g/8 oz gooseberries
75 ml/3 fl oz water
25 g/1 oz butter
1 tbsp chopped fresh fennel
Sugar to taste
Salt and freshly ground pepper

Wash, top and tail the gooseberries then place them in a saucepan with the water and cook until soft. Either leave them whole or purée the sauce.

Add the remaining ingredients, heat through and serve.

SUITABLE FOR FREEZING.

Plum

Substitute a little port for some of the wine if you prefer. Serve with gammon, turkey or venison.

MAKES ABOUT 450 ML/¾ PT

450 g/1 lb plums, stones removed
300 ml/½ pt white wine
2 tbsp tarragon vinegar
40 g/1½ oz sugar
1 tbsp cornflour
Salt and freshly ground white pepper

Skin the plums, if liked, then put them in a saucepan with the wine and vinegar. Simmer gently until tender then sieve or liquidize to a purée. Add the sugar and simmer without the lid until reduced by a quarter.

Blend the cornflour with a little water, stir in some of the hot liquid then stir this mixture into the pan. Bring to the boil, stirring, and add seasoning and cook for about 2 minutes until thickened. Serve either hot or cold.

THIS WILL FREEZE BETTER BEFORE THE CORNFLOUR IS ADDED.

Starfruit and Pineapple

A truly fruity sauce, which goes well with duck.

MAKES ABOUT 600 ML/1 PT

1 small leek, trimmed and finely shredded
450 ml/¾ pt medium-sweet white wine
50 ml/2 fl oz cider vinegar
1 small starfruit, thinly sliced
50 g/2 oz tinned small pineapple pieces
2 tsp wholegrain mustard
25 g/1 oz granulated sugar
2 tbsp cornflour

Put the leek, wine, vinegar and starfruit in a pan, cutting the pieces smaller if necessary. Cover and cook gently to soften the leek and cook the starfruit a little – this shouldn't take more than 10 minutes, depending on the ripeness of the fruit. Remove the pan from the heat and stir in the pineapple.

Blend the mustard, sugar and cornflour with a little water. Stir in some of the liquid from the pan then return this mixture to the pan. Bring to the boil, stirring, and cook until thickened, about 3 minutes. Serve hot or cold.

NOT SUITABLE FOR FREEZING.

Pineapple and Green Pepper

A good sauce to serve with duck, pork or bacon joints.

MAKES ABOUT 450 ML/¾ PT

25 g/1 oz butter
1 small onion, chopped
75 g/3 oz green pepper, deseeded and sliced
400 g/14 oz can pineapple rings
About 150 ml/¼ pt chicken stock
1 tbsp cornflour
1 tbsp lemon juice
Salt and pepper

Melt the butter in a pan and fry the onion for 3 minutes until softened. Stir in the green pepper and cook for 2 minutes or until softened. Remove the pan from the heat.

Drain and reserve the pineapple juice and cut up the pineapple rings. Make up the juice to 300 ml/½ pt with the chicken stock and add to the onion and pepper.

Blend the cornflour with the lemon juice and some of the stock from the pan then add this mixture to the pan. Bring to the boil, stirring, and cook for 3 minutes. Add the pineapple pieces, heat through, season to taste and serve.

THIS WILL FREEZE FOR A SHORT TIME ONLY.

Spiced Ginger

A sweet, slightly sharp, spicy sauce ideal for serving with pork, chicken or cooked bacon joints.

MAKES 300 ML/½ PT

40 g/1½ oz butter or margarine
1 onion, chopped
¼ tsp ground coriander
¼ tsp ground ginger or
1 tsp grated fresh ginger root
2 tbsp cornflour
300 ml/½ pt chicken stock
1 tsp lemon juice
50 g/2 oz chopped preserved ginger
Salt and pepper

Melt the butter or margarine in a pan, add the onion and cook without browning until softened. Remove the pan from the heat and stir in the coriander and ginger.

Blend the cornflour with a little of the stock then stir in the remainder and pour it into the pan.

Return the pan to the heat and stir until the sauce thickens. Bring to the boil and cook for 2 minutes. Stir in the remaining ingredients, adding salt and pepper to taste.

SUITABLE FOR FREEZING.

CHAPTER NINE

Cold Sauces and Relishes
~

COLD SAUCES AND RELISHES 57

Aïoli

This garlic mayonnaise can be served with vegetables, as a salad dressing or as a dip. If you add parsley it is good with scampi, fish or chicken goujons.

MAKES 300 ML/½ PT

4 cloves garlic, crushed
2 egg yolks
Pinch of salt and pepper
300 ml/½ pt olive oil
Lemon juice (optional)

Crush the garlic until really smooth then put it in a bowl. Add the egg yolks and salt and beat well. Gradually beat in the oil, as for mayonnaise (see page 22).

If the mixture becomes too thick add a little lemon juice or warm water. Taste and adjust the seasoning.

NOT SUITABLE FOR FREEZING.

Cold Curry

This is the sauce to mix with cold cooked chicken for either Coronation Chicken or Chicken Elizabeth. It can also be served over hard-boiled eggs as a starter.

**MAKES 600 ML/1 PT
(ENOUGH FOR 2 COOKED CHICKENS)**

1 tbsp oil
1 small onion, finely chopped
3 tsp curry powder
1 tsp tomato purée
150 ml/¼ pt water
1 tbsp mango chutney
150 ml/¼ pt plain yogurt
300 ml/½ pt mayonnaise (see page 22)
2 tbsp single cream (optional)

Place the oil and onion in a saucepan and cook gently for about 5 minutes until the onion is softened. Stir in the curry powder and fry for about 1 minute. Add the tomato purée, water and mango chutney and simmer for about 5 minutes.

Sieve the sauce and leave to cool. Place in a bowl and gradually beat in the yogurt, making sure it is well blended between each addition. Fold in the mayonnaise and the cream, if using.

NOT SUITABLE FOR FREEZING.

Ravigote

A mayonnaise-based sauce for serving with cold chicken, beef or salmon.

MAKES ABOUT 300 ML/½ PT

300 ml/½ pt mayonnaise (see page 22)
1 tsp Dijon mustard
1 tbsp capers, finely chopped
2 tbsp chopped fresh herbs, such as tarragon, chives and parsley
2 spring onions, trimmed and finely chopped
1 hard-boiled egg, finely chopped
Dash of Worcestershire sauce

Put the mayonnaise in a bowl and mix in the remaining ingredients. Leave to stand for a while to allow the flavours to blend. Chill before serving.

NOT SUITABLE FOR FREEZING.

Rémoulade

A classic mayonnaise sauce to serve with fish or to stir into a fish and pasta salad.

MAKES 300 ML/½ PT

300 ml/½ pt mayonnaise (see page 22)
1 tsp Dijon mustard
1 tbsp capers, finely chopped
1 tbsp finely chopped gherkins
1 tbsp finely chopped fresh tarragon
1 tsp anchovy fillets, pounded, or anchovy essence
1 hard-boiled egg, finely chopped
Salt and freshly ground pepper

Place the mayonnaise in a bowl, stir in the remaining ingredients and adjust the seasoning to taste. Serve chilled to allow the flavours to mingle.

NOT SUITABLE FOR FREEZING.

Quick Lemon and Caper

Serve with fish or as a relish for a fondue, or thin down a little and use as a dressing for pasta or salad.

MAKES 300 ML/½ PT

300 ml/½ pt sour cream or crème fraîche
2 tbsp capers, chopped
Grated rind of 1 lemon
Salt and freshly ground white pepper
A little chopped fresh parsley

Place the sour cream or crème fraîche in a bowl and whisk with a fork. Add the remaining ingredients. Chill slightly before serving.

QUICK TO MAKE. NO NEED TO FREEZE.

Tonnata (Tuna Fish Mayonnaise)

A delicious and versatile Italian sauce. Serve over cold cooked chicken, hard-boiled eggs or with veal, or try stirring it into a pasta salad.

MAKES ABOUT 225 ML/8 FL OZ

175 g/6 fl oz mayonnaise (see page 22)
100 g/3½ oz can tuna fish, well drained
Small can of anchovy fillets, well drained
Freshly ground pepper
2 tsp lemon juice, or to taste

Place the mayonnaise and tuna in a blender or food processor with 3 of the anchovy fillets. Blend until smooth, then add a little pepper and lemon juice to taste.

Serve garnished with the remaining anchovy fillets.

NOT SUITABLE FOR FREEZING.

Tartare

Serve as an accompaniment to fish. Use half mayonnaise and half yogurt for a lighter, healthier sauce.

MAKES 150 ML/¼ PT

150 ml/¼ pt mayonnaise (see page 22)
1 tsp capers
1 mini gherkin
½ tsp each of finely chopped fresh parsley, tarragon and chives
Salt and pepper

Place the mayonnaise in a sauceboat. Chop the capers and gherkin fairly small and add to the mayonnaise with the herbs and seasoning to taste. If the sauce is too thick add a little vinegar from the capers. Serve fairly soon after being made.

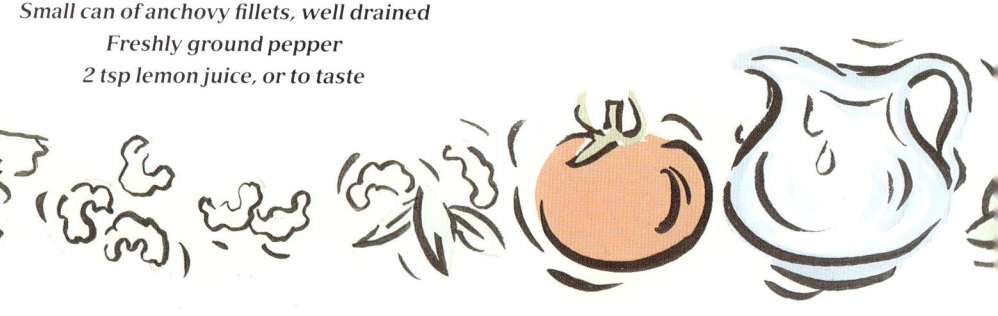

NOT SUITABLE FOR FREEZING.

Cranberry

A traditional sauce for turkey, which goes well with pork, venison and lamb, too. The rind and juice of an orange could also be added.

MAKES ABOUT 300 ML/½ PT

225 g/8 oz fresh cranberries
150 ml/¼ pt water
125 g/4 oz sugar, or to taste
¼ tsp ground mace (optional)
Salt and pepper
Small knob of butter

Place the cranberries in a saucepan with the water and cook gently for about 10 minutes until softened. Add sufficient sugar to sweeten, with the mace, if using, seasoning and a small knob of butter. Serve either hot or cold.

IDEAL MADE IN ADVANCE AND FROZEN.

Mint

The only real sauce to serve with roast lamb. The quantities here have to be a bit vague, as it depends so much upon personal preference. I feel the mint should be quite solid so the vinegar just floats on the surface.

MAKES ABOUT 150 ML/¼ PT

Handful of fresh mint
3–4 tsp sugar, to taste
4 tbsp white wine vinegar

Wash and dry the mint well then chop it finely. Place it in a sauceboat with some sugar, stir it around and leave for a while to allow the sugar to soften. Pour on sufficient vinegar to float the mint.

Alternatively the sugar can be dissolved in the vinegar by warming it; allow it to cool then pour it over the mint.

FREEZE FRESH MINT LEAVES WHEN SEASONAL.

Tangy Redcurrant Relish

This sauce is made very quickly using redcurrant jelly. If you find it too sweet, add a little extra vinegar. Serve with lamb, gammon joints and bacon chops.

MAKES ABOUT 125 ML/4 FL OZ

6 tbsp redcurrant jelly
1½ tbsp red wine vinegar

Place the jelly in a small saucepan over a low heat and stir until it begins to melt. Add the vinegar and continue stirring until the lumps dissolve. Bring to the boil and simmer for 2 minutes to reduce the sauce a little. Serve hot or cold.

FREEZING NOT RECOMMENDED.

Sour Cream and Chive

This sauce could also be made with yogurt or crème fraîche, and other herbs could be substituted for the chives.

MAKES 150 ML/¼ PT

150 ml/¼ pt sour cream
1 tbsp lemon juice
2 tbsp finely chopped fresh chives
Tabasco sauce
Salt and freshly ground pepper
Paprika pepper (optional)

Combine the sour cream with the lemon juice and chives in a bowl. Add a few drops of Tabasco and salt and pepper to taste. Spoon into a serving dish and, if liked, sprinkle over a little paprika pepper.

FREEZING NOT RECOMMENDED.
SOUR CREAM DOES NOT FREEZE WELL.

Waldorf

This makes a good accompaniment to beetroot or tomato in jelly, and may also be served with cold meats.

MAKES 300 ML/½ PT

1 dessert apple, cored and diced
25 g/1 oz walnuts, chopped
1 stick celery, finely chopped
2 tsp chopped fresh parsley or chives
250 ml/8 fl oz sour cream
50 ml/2 fl oz mayonnaise (see page 22)
Salt and pepper

Mix all the ingredients together, adding salt and pepper to taste.

NOT SUITABLE FOR FREEZING.

Horseradish

The correct way to make this sauce is to grate your own horseradish. Grated horseradish can be bought in jars but the flavour is not as good. Use a mixture of yogurt and sour cream in this recipe to make it less rich, if preferred.

MAKES ABOUT 175 ML/6 FL OZ

5 tbsp freshly grated horseradish
150 ml/¼ pt whipping cream or sour cream
Salt and pepper
Pinch of sugar
A little made English mustard

Mix all the ingredients together. Serve with beef.

SUITABLE FOR FREEZING.

CHAPTER TEN

Marinades and Dressings

~

Avocado Dressing

This quick sauce should be prepared at the last minute as avocado can discolour quickly. Serve with fish, salads or jacket potatoes.

MAKES ABOUT 150 ML/¼ PT

1 ripe avocado
1 tbsp lemon juice
4 tbsp French dressing (see page 62)
2 tbsp chopped fresh chives
1 tsp Tabasco sauce

Peel and stone the avocado, place it in a bowl and mash with a fork until smooth. Add the lemon juice then add all the remaining ingredients.

NOT SUITABLE FOR FREEZING.

French Dressing (Vinaigrette)

This is a useful item to have in the refrigerator and it keeps well. Make it in a screw-top jar with a plastic lid to prevent corrosion from the vinegar. Heavy vinegars are too harsh, so use cider, herb or wine vinegar instead. The flavour can be varied by using different oils, sweeteners and mustards. This is the basic recipe.

MAKES 125 ML/4 FL OZ

Pinch each of salt, pepper, caster sugar and dry mustard
8 tbsp oil
2 tbsp vinegar
1 clove garlic, crushed (optional)

Place the seasonings in a screw-top jar, blend in a little of the oil then add the remainder with the vinegar. Shake well. Chopped fresh herbs can be added.

NOT SUITABLE FOR FREEZING.

Boiled Salad Dressing

A sharp, creamy dressing, good with potatoes and eggs. Use a wholegrain mustard if preferred.

MAKES 300 ML/½ PT

1 tbsp light soft brown sugar
2 tsp plain flour
1 tsp salt
2 tsp Dijon mustard
150 ml/¼ pt white malt vinegar
4 tbsp water
25 g/1 oz unsalted butter
150 ml/¼ pt creamy milk, or half milk and half single cream

Mix the dry ingredients together, add the mustard then blend in the vinegar and water. Place in a heavy saucepan and bring to the boil. Reduce to a simmer and cook, stirring, for about 10 minutes, adding more water if necessary. Remove the pan from the heat and add the butter and milk.

NOT SUITABLE FOR FREEZING.

Sour Cream Dressing

The herbs in this dressing should be varied; try using tarragon instead of marjoram, for example. A nice sauce to serve with jacket potatoes or tossed into pasta salads.

MAKES 150 ML/¼ PT

150 ml/¼ pt sour cream
1 tbsp lemon juice or French dressing (see page 62)
1 tbsp each of finely chopped fresh parsley, chives and marjoram
1 tsp Tabasco sauce
Salt and freshly ground black pepper

Place the sour cream in a bowl then stir in all the remaining ingredients, adding seasoning to taste. Serve chilled.

NOT SUITABLE FOR FREEZING.

Blue Cheese Dressing

This can be made with any blue cheese and any combination of yogurt, mayonnaise, crème fraîche or sour cream. Care should be taken, however, if the blue cheese is on the acid side, as it may clash with sharp yogurt. Ideal for salads and jacket potatoes.

MAKES 450 ML/¾ PT

125 g/4 oz light cream cheese
125 g/4 oz Mycella, Danish or other blue cheese
6 tbsp mayonnaise (see page 22)
1–2 tbsp milk
1 tbsp chopped fresh parsley
1 tbsp chopped fresh chives
Freshly ground pepper

Place the cheeses in a bowl and mash well, then gradually blend in the mayonnaise and milk.

A food processor could be used for this. Add the remaining ingredients, with a little more milk if necessary to give the required consistency.

NOT SUITABLE FOR FREEZING.

Watercress and Walnut

An unusual dressing to serve over green salads or rice.

MAKES ABOUT 300 ML/½ PT

1 spring onion, finely chopped
1 tsp creamed horseradish sauce (see page 60)
200 ml/7 fl oz crème fraîche
5 tbsp milk
Salt and pepper
25 g/1 oz walnuts, chopped
½ bunch watercress, stalks removed

Mix together the spring onion, horseradish sauce, crème fraîche and milk. Season to taste. Add remaining ingredients and chill the sauce for 30 minutes before serving.

NOT SUITABLE FOR FREEZING.

White Wine Marinade

Use this uncooked marinade with chicken, fish or turkey, and add some of it to the sauce for flavour.

MAKES 775 ML/1 PT 6 FL OZ

6 peppercorns
1 carrot, finely chopped
1 small onion, finely chopped
1 small clove garlic, peeled (optional)
1 celery stalk, chopped
Sprig of parsley
Sprig of thyme
1 bay leaf
600 ml/1 pt dry white wine
175 ml/6 fl oz oil

Mix all the ingredients together, add the meat to be marinated then cover and leave in the refrigerator for up to 12 hours (about 3 hours for firm fish). Turn the meat occasionally.

NOT SUITABLE FOR FREEZING.

Tomato Dressing

A good dressing to make when tomatoes are plentiful. Serve over cold fish or vegetables and substitute other herbs, if liked.

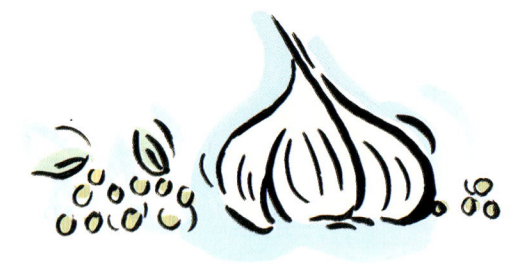

MAKES 300 ML/½ PT

350 g/12 oz fresh ripe tomatoes
5 tbsp olive oil
2 tbsp white wine vinegar
1 tsp tomato purée
1 clove garlic, crushed
1 tbsp lemon juice
Salt and freshly ground black pepper
1 tbsp chopped fresh basil

Purée the tomatoes in a blender or food processor then strain through a sieve. Mix in all the remaining ingredients. Chill before serving so the flavours develop.

NOT SUITABLE FOR FREEZING.

Thousand Island Dressing

MAKES ABOUT 300 ML/½ PT

150 ml/¼ pt mayonnaise (see page 22)
150 ml/¼ pt crème fraîche or thick plain yogurt
1 tbsp cider vinegar
Pinch of paprika
2 tbsp tomato ketchup
6 pimento-stuffed olives, chopped
2 tsp chopped fresh chives
1 tsp chopped fresh parsley
1 clove garlic, crushed
Salt and freshly ground pepper
A little milk (optional)

Mix all the ingredients together then cover and chill to allow the flavour to develop. Add a little milk for a thinner sauce.

NOT SUITABLE FOR FREEZING.

Red Wine Marinade

Use this for marinating beef, game or pork.

MAKES 300 ML/½ PT

4 tbsp oil
1 onion, sliced
1 carrot, sliced
1 stick celery, sliced
1 clove garlic, sliced
1 bottle red wine
100 ml/4 fl oz red wine vinegar
8 juniper berries, slightly crushed
10 peppercorns
Sprig of parsley
Sprig of thyme
1 bay leaf

Heat the oil in a pan, sauté the vegetables slowly for about 5 minutes then add all the remaining ingredients. Simmer for about 15 minutes then allow to cool. Pour it over the meat to be marinated, in a container that will not be affected by acid and that will fit into the refrigerator. Make sure the meat is completely covered with the marinade and leave for 2–3 days.

Use about 150 ml/¼ pt of the marinade to make a sauce, making it up to 600 ml/1 pt with stock. Or use all the marinade when making a richer sauce, such as bourguignonne (see page 28).

NOT SUITABLE FOR FREEZING.

Lemon Marinade

Use to marinate fish; any that is left over could be added to a sauce accompanying the dish.

MAKES ABOUT 150 ML/¼ PT

4 tbsp olive oil
4 tbsp lemon juice
2 tbsp chopped fresh parsley
1 clove garlic, crushed
Salt and freshly ground black pepper

Mix all the ingredients together. Toss cubes of fish in the marinade and leave for 30 minutes before cooking.

NOT SUITABLE FOR FREEZING.

Cocktail

A very simple traditional recipe to serve with prawns or other fish. It could also be used as a dip for scampi or stirred into pasta.

MAKES 300 ML/½ PT

300 ml/½ pt mayonnaise (see page 22)
1 tsp tomato purée
A few drops of Tabasco sauce

Place all the ingredients in a bowl and mix well together.

NOT SUITABLE FOR FREEZING.

Spicy Marinade

Use this for cubes of meat or lamb chops; it's particularly good with meat that is to be barbecued. Any left-over marinade could be added to barbecue sauce and cooked for a short while.

MAKES 125 G/4 OZ

2 spring onions, finely chopped
2 shallots, finely chopped
½ tsp salt
½ tsp ground cumin
½ tsp ground ginger
½ tsp ground coriander
½ tsp freshly ground black pepper
Pinch of paprika
4 tbsp olive oil

Pound the spring onions and shallots with the salt to form a paste. Add the spices then gradually blend in the olive oil. Rub into the meat to be marinated, and leave for several hours.

NOT SUITABLE FOR FREEZING.

CHAPTER ELEVEN

Creams, Custards and Milk Sauces

~

Rich Orange Cream

A rich sauce to serve over strawberries, pancakes or fruit pies.

MAKES ABOUT 300 ML/½ PT

Finely grated rind of 1 orange
4 tbsp orange juice
3 egg yolks
75 g/3 oz caster sugar
150 ml/¼ pt double cream
1–2 tbsp Grand Marnier (optional)

Place the orange rind and juice, egg yolks and sugar in a mixing bowl and whisk together.

Put the bowl over a saucepan of hot water and keep the water simmering, but not boiling. Whisk the mixture until really thick and pale in colour. Remove the bowl from the heat and continue whisking until cold.

When the mixture is completely cold, add the cream and the liqueur, if using, then whisk again until the desired consistency is reached. Serve slightly chilled.

NOT SUITABLE FOR FREEZING.

Chestnut

This delicious sauce does thicken up a bit on standing, which is why thin double cream needs to be used (single cream would not be creamy enough). The Cointreau does round the sauce off, but other liqueurs could be substituted, if preferred.

MAKES 600 ML/1 PT

425 g/15 oz can unsweetened chestnut purée
150 ml/¼ pt caramel sauce (see page 72)
150 ml/¼ pt thin double cream, of pouring consistency
1 tbsp Cointreau (optional)

Place the chestnut purée in a saucepan over a very low heat and stir to break up the lumps a little, being careful that it does not burn. Remove from the heat and gradually blend in the caramel sauce.

Return to the heat for a short while so the mixture loosens up; use a potato masher if necessary. It could be sieved to give a smoother sauce. Stir in the cream and the liqueur, if using.

Can be served hot or cold.

THIS WILL FREEZE FOR UP TO 1 MONTH.

Chantilly Cream

A topping for puddings, pies, etc. The egg white gives a lighter result.

MAKES ABOUT 175 ML/6 FL OZ

175 ml/6 fl oz double cream
Few drops of vanilla essence
1 tbsp icing sugar, sieved
1 egg white (optional)

Chill the cream well then pour it into a bowl and whisk with the vanilla and icing sugar until light and fluffy. If using the egg white, whisk it until stiff then carefully fold it into the cream.

WILL NOT FREEZE.

Rum and Raisin

Serve this sweet white sauce with plain steamed puddings.

MAKES 450 ML/¾ PT

25 g/1 oz cornflour
25 g/1 oz caster sugar
450 ml/¾ pt milk
50 g/2 oz seeded raisins, chopped
3 tbsp rum
2–3 tbsp single cream

Blend the cornflour and caster sugar in a bowl with a little of the cold milk. Heat the remaining milk just to boiling point then stir it into the blended mixture.

Rinse the saucepan out then pour in the sauce. Bring to the boil, stirring, and simmer for 3 minutes. Remove the pan from the heat and stir in the raisins, rum and cream. Serve either hot or cold.

FREEZE WITHOUT THE RUM OR CREAM.

Mousseline

This sauce is served warm and is delicious with Christmas pudding.

MAKES 175 ML/6 FL OZ

2 eggs
125 g/4 oz caster sugar
4 tbsp dry sherry or orange juice

Place all the ingredients in a bowl set over a pan of boiling water. Whisk until the mixture is thick and the whisk leaves a trail on the surface.

Serve warm within 1 hour of making as it will separate.

NOT SUITABLE FOR FREEZING.

Creamy Syrup

A slightly different sweet, buttery sauce. You can omit some of the cream and substitute brandy or rum, if preferred. Serve with hot steamed puddings or ice cream.

MAKES ABOUT 175 ML/6 FL OZ

125 g/4 oz butter, softened
150 g/5 oz icing sugar, sieved
125 g/4 oz golden syrup
4 tbsp single cream
Vanilla essence

Cream the butter and icing sugar until light and fluffy, then beat in the syrup, cream and vanilla essence to taste. Chill slightly before serving.

NOT RECOMMENDED FOR FREEZING.

Sherry

Serve with Christmas pudding or any steamed or baked pudding.

MAKES ABOUT 150 ML/¼ PT

4 tbsp medium sherry
2 egg yolks
2 tsp caster sugar
3 tbsp single cream

Place the sherry, egg yolks and sugar in a bowl and place this over a pan of hot water. Whisk well until the sauce becomes light and frothy.

Remove the bowl from the heat and whisk in the cream. Keep warm until ready to serve, making sure it does not get too hot as the cream will separate.

NOT SUITABLE FOR FREEZING.

Chocolate Custard

This is a basic cornflour and cocoa custard.

MAKES 450 ML/¾ PT

2 tbsp custard powder
3 tbsp cocoa powder
450 ml/¾ pt milk
2–3 knobs of butter
Sugar to taste

Mix the custard powder and cocoa in a basin with some of the cold milk. Heat the remaining milk just to the boil then pour it over the blended mixture, stirring. Rinse out the saucepan and return the custard to the pan.

Bring to the boil, stirring, and cook for 3 minutes. Add butter and sugar to taste. Serve either hot or cold.

SUITABLE FOR FREEZING.

Confectioner's Custard

Flour is used to thicken this custard, thus reducing the number of egg yolks required. Vanilla sugar could be used instead of vanilla essence. Use as a filling for cakes or fruit flans.

MAKES 300 ML/½ PT

300 ml/½ pt milk
Few drops of vanilla essence
2 egg yolks
50 g/2 oz caster sugar
25 g/1 oz plain flour

Pour the milk into a saucepan, bring to the boil then remove from the heat and add the vanilla essence.

Whisk the egg yolks in a bowl with the sugar until thick and creamy, then fold in the flour. Gradually stir the milk into this mixture. Rinse out the saucepan and pour back the custard. Cook over a low heat, stirring, for 1–2 minutes to cook the flour. The custard should become thick enough to coat the back of a spoon.

SUITABLE FOR FREEZING, BUT BEAT WELL ON THAWING.

Note: A little cream may be added if the custard becomes a bit too thick.

Quick Custard

Serve over puddings, fruit salads or stewed fruit.

MAKES 300 ML/½ PT

2 tbsp custard powder
300 ml/½ pt milk
1 tbsp sugar

Blend the custard powder with a little of the cold milk to give a smooth paste. Bring the remaining milk almost to the boil then pour it over the blended paste. Rinse out the saucepan, return the milk to the pan and bring to the boil, stirring all the time. Cook for 2 minutes until the custard has thickened. Add sugar to taste.

Serve either hot or cold.

QUICK TO MAKE, SO NOT WORTH FREEZING.

Zabaglione

This wonderful, richly flavored Marsala sauce can be eaten with crisp delicate cookies, or served with fresh fruit salad.

MAKES ABOUT 1 CUP

4 egg yolks
⅓ cup golden caster sugar
6 tbsp Marsala or other strong dessert wine

Place the egg yolks in a large bowl with the sugar. Put the bowl over a pan of simmering water, being careful that the water does not touch the base of the bowl. Blend the mixture with a whisk; then, when it begins to come together start whisking in the Marsala.

Continue whisking until the mixture is pale, creamy and thick. Care must be taken not to let the water in the pan underneath boil.

Pour into glasses, and serve while still warm.

NOT SUITABLE FOR FREEZING.

Hot Chocolate

Chocolate sauce is always popular and this one is easy to make as it is thickened with cornstarch. Serve over hot sponge puddings, ice cream or fruit.

MAKES ABOUT ¾ CUP

2 squares dark chocolate, broken into pieces
1 tbsp superfine sugar
⅔ cup milk
3 tsp cornstarch
4 tbsp water
Knob of butter
Vanilla extract

Place the chocolate, sugar and milk in a small saucepan. Heat gently until the sugar has dissolved, and the chocolate has melted.

Blend the cornstarch with the water, and stir in some of the hot milk mixture; then return it to the pan and bring gently to the boil, stirring all the time. Add the butter and vanilla, and cook for 1 minute. Serve.

SUITABLE FOR FREEZING. LET COOL, COVERED WITH PLASTIC WRAP TO PREVENT A SKIN FORMING, THEN FREEZE IN A SUITABLE CONTAINER.

VARIATIONS

Chocolate and Orange – add the grated rind of 1 orange.
Chocolate and Rum – add 1–2 tbsp rum.

Sweet White

This is an easy sauce to make and versatile, too, as a number of flavorings can be added.

MAKES ABOUT 2½ CUPS

3 tbsp cornstarch
2½ cups milk
2 tbsp sugar
1 tbsp butter
A little vanilla extract

Blend the cornstarch in a basin with a little of the milk. Heat the remaining milk just to boiling point, then stir it into the blended cornstarch. Rinse out the saucepan, return the sauce to the pan, and boil for 1 minute, stirring all the time. Add the sugar, butter and vanilla or other flavorings.

VARIATIONS

Chocolate – add 1 tbsp cocoa powder to the cornstarch and use 1 oz sugar.
Coffee – add 3 tsp instant coffee to the cornstarch and use extra sugar to taste.
Lemon or Orange – add the finely grated rind of ½ lemon/orange and the juice of 1 lemon/orange, plus extra sugar.
Ginger – add ½ tsp ground ginger mixed with chopped crystallized ginger, and cook slightly longer to blend in the ground ginger.

SUITABLE FOR FREEZING.

CHAPTER TWELVE

The Sweeter Sauces

~

Butterscotch

This is ideal to serve over ice-cream sundaes, pancakes and steamed chocolate pudding.

MAKES 300 ML/½ PT

125 g/4 oz golden syrup
125 g/4 oz light soft brown sugar
25 g/1 oz butter
2 tbsp boiling water
½–1 tsp vanilla essence
4 tbsp single cream

Place the syrup, sugar and butter in a heavy-based saucepan. Heat gently until the sugar has dissolved, stirring occasionally, then bring to the boil and boil steadily for 3 minutes. Remove the pan from the heat and very slowly add the boiling water. Mix well then allow to cool slightly.

Stir in the vanilla then add the cream a spoonful at a time, mixing in each addition.

Serve either hot or cold, adding extra cream to thin the sauce if necessary.

WILL KEEP IN THE REFRIGERATOR.

Caramel

This useful sauce keeps in a screw-top jar for ages, so make double the recipe if you like. Great care should be taken when boiling the sugar.

MAKES ABOUT 300 ML/½ PT

175 g/6 oz caster sugar
150 ml/¼ pt cold water
125 ml/4 fl oz warm water

Place the sugar in a medium-sized heavy-based saucepan and add the cold water. Heat gently to dissolve the sugar, making sure there are no sugar crystals up the sides of the pan. When the sugar has completely dissolved, bring to the boil.

Continue boiling until the sugar becomes a pale golden colour. Watch it constantly, as if it becomes too dark the caramel will be bitter.

Quickly cover your hand with a tea towel then pick up the pan and immediately dip the base of it in cold water to stop the cooking. Still keeping your hand covered, very slowly pour in the warm water, then return the pan to the stove to dissolve any caramel on the base. Allow to cool before storing in a screw-top glass jar.

WILL KEEP IN A STORE-CUPBOARD.

Hot Fudge

A simple sauce made with store-cupboard ingredients. Serve with ice cream and steamed puddings.

MAKES ABOUT 175 ML/6 FL OZ

175 g/6 oz light soft brown sugar
4 tbsp golden syrup
50 g/2 oz unsalted butter
8 tbsp evaporated milk

Place all the ingredients in a heavy saucepan and heat gently for 5 minutes until they are well blended. Do not allow to boil.

WILL KEEP IN THE REFRIGERATOR FOR A FEW DAYS.

VARIATIONS

Add 25 g/1 oz chopped dates, 40 g/1½ oz chopped walnuts or Brazils or 50 g/2 oz grated plain chocolate.

Cream and Honey

A quick sauce to serve over Christmas pudding.

MAKES ABOUT 300 ML/½ PT

300 ml/½ pt double cream
2 tbsp thick honey
2 tbsp rum or brandy

Place the cream and honey in a basin. Just before serving put the basin over a saucepan of hot water and heat gently for 3 minutes to blend the ingredients. Remove the pan from the heat and stir in the rum or brandy. Serve at once.

NOT SUITABLE FOR FREEZING.

Peach and Passion

A little cream could be added, if liked. Serve over pavlova or ice cream.

MAKES ABOUT 150 ML/¼ PT

2 ripe peaches
6 passion fruit
2 tbsp dry sherry
Icing sugar, sieved

Peel and stone the peaches, then sieve them into a bowl. Halve the passion fruit, scoop out the seeds and add to the peach purée. Stir in the sherry and sufficient icing sugar to sweeten.

SUITABLE FOR FREEZING.

Fluffy Lemon

Serve over hot pancakes or with Christmas Pudding, for a change.

MAKES ABOUT 150 ML/¼ PT

75 g/3 oz unsalted butter, softened
225 g/8 oz icing sugar, sieved
Rind and juice of 1 large lemon
1 egg yolk

Beat the butter until really soft then gradually beat in the icing sugar with the lemon rind and juice. Continue beating until smooth then beat in the egg yolk.

Depending on the size of the lemon it may be necessary to add extra icing sugar.

NOT SUITABLE FOR FREEZING.

Jam and Arrowroot

Use any jam for this. For a thinner sauce, boil together 4 tbsp jam, 4 tbsp water, 2 tsp sugar and the juice of ½ lemon.

MAKES ABOUT 100 ML/4 FL OZ

5 tbsp jam
150 ml/¼ pt water
1 tbsp lemon juice
1½ tsp arrowroot

Put the jam and water in a saucepan and heat gently to dissolve, then add the lemon juice. Blend the arrowroot with a little water and add to the melted jam. Bring to the boil, stirring, and cook until it thickens and clears. Sieve to obtain a smooth sauce, if preferred.

FREEZING NOT RECOMMENDED.

Chocolate

A rich chocolate sauce that can be made in advance.

MAKES 150 ML/¼ PT

125 g/4 oz plain chocolate
1 tbsp sugar
150 ml/¼ pt hot water
Knob of butter
Few drops of vanilla essence (optional)

Break the chocolate into pieces and place in a saucepan with the sugar and hot water. Heat gently to melt the chocolate and dissolve the sugar, stirring occasionally.

Raise the heat to allow the sauce to bubble gently and reduce a little, until it becomes syrupy. Stir in the butter and the vanilla, if using. A little brandy or rum could also be added but not too much in case it masks the flavour of the chocolate.

KEEPS FOR 2–3 WEEKS WITHOUT FREEZING.

Quick Toffee

MAKES ABOUT 175 ML/6 FL OZ

225 g/8 oz toffees or caramels
6 tbsp water

Place the ingredients in a small saucepan. Stir over a low heat until melted.

VARIATION

Add 4 tbsp chopped mixed nuts.

WILL KEEP FOR 1–2 WEEKS IN REFRIGERATOR.

Hot Ginger

Serve with ice cream, pears or melon or with a green fruit salad.

MAKES 300 ML/½ PT

4 tsp cornflour
300 ml/½ pt water
2 tbsp clear honey
½ tsp ground ginger
1–2 tbsp chopped preserved ginger
2 tbsp syrup from the ginger jar

Blend the cornflour with a little of the water. Heat the remaining water. Add the honey and ground ginger. Blend a little of this liquid into the cornflour and mix into the saucepan. Cook for 3 minutes. Add the chopped ginger and syrup to the sauce.

SUITABLE FOR FREEZING.

Raspberry Coulis

A fruit coulis is a fruit purée which is strained to remove skin and pips. The firmer soft fruits such as blackcurrants and cherries need cooking first. Fruit purées may also be thickened with arrowroot.

MAKES ABOUT 425 ML/¾ PT

450 g/1 lb fresh or frozen raspberries
Icing sugar to sweeten
Lemon juice

Pick the fruit over then, using a plastic sieve or a food processor, sieve or process the raspberries. Strain out the pips if necessary.

Sweeten with icing sugar and add a little lemon juice to bring out the flavour.

WHEN THERE IS A GLUT OF RASPBERRIES MAKE A LARGE QUANTITY OF COULIS FOR THE FREEZER, PUT IT IN SUITABLE PLASTIC CONTAINERS AND FREEZE.

Note: This is a good way of freezing strawberries, or they can just be mashed, to save space, then puréed when required.

Melba

A good sauce to make and freeze when raspberries are plentiful.

MAKES ABOUT 150 ML/¼ PT

4 tbsp redcurrant jelly
75 g/3 oz sugar
150 ml/¼ pt fresh raspberry purée (see page 74)
2 tsp arrowroot
1 tbsp cold water

Melt the redcurrant jelly in a saucepan then add the sugar and raspberry purée.

Blend together the arrowroot and water and add to the pan. Bring to the boil, stirring, until the mixture thickens and clears. Serve either hot or cold.

SUITABLE FOR FREEZING.

Blackberry

Other fruits, such as blackcurrants, redcurrants, gooseberries, plums and peaches, could be cooked in the same way. Serve over pavlova, ice cream or other fruit.

MAKES ABOUT 300 ML/½ PT

225 g/8 oz blackberries
50 g/2 oz caster sugar
1½ tbsp cornflour
6 tbsp water
A little lemon juice (optional)

Place the blackberries in a saucepan with the sugar and water. Cover and cook gently for a few minutes then either purée the fruit or leave it whole.

Blend the cornflour with a little water and add it to the fruit. Bring to the boil, stirring, and simmer for 3 minutes. Allow to cool, then add a little lemon juice, if liked.

SUITABLE FOR FREEZING.

Economical Chocolate

This version is made with cocoa powder and is thinner than the previous recipe. Add a knob of butter for a richer sauce.

MAKES 300 ML/½ PT

2 tbsp sugar
25 g/1 oz cocoa
300 ml/½ pt water
Knob of butter (optional)
Few drops of vanilla essence or 1 tbsp brandy or rum

Mix the sugar and cocoa together in a saucepan, blend with a little of the water until smooth then stir in the remainder. Bring the sauce to the boil and boil for 5 minutes to reduce it. Stir in the butter, if using, and allow to cool. Then add the vanilla essence, brandy or rum.

SUITABLE FOR FREEZING.

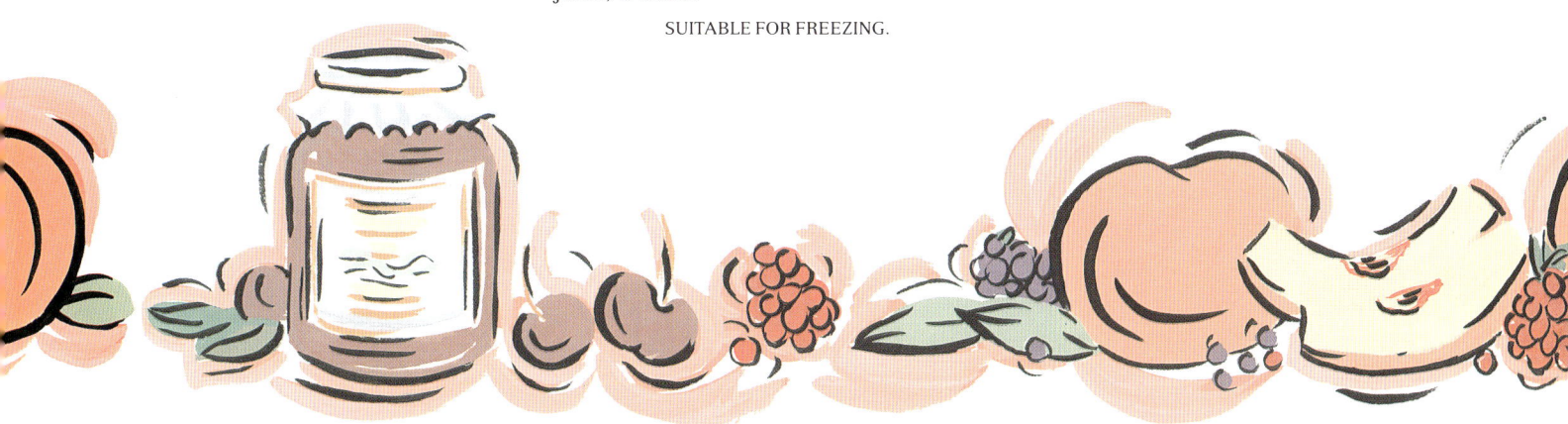

Orange Liqueur

A quick last-minute sauce to serve with pancakes, steamed puddings and ice cream or over meringues.

MAKES ABOUT 175 ML/6 FL OZ

175 g/6 oz orange marmalade
1 tbsp caster sugar
Juice of 1 orange
2 tbsp Cointreau or Grand Marnier
3 tsp arrowroot
Knob of butter

Chop the marmalade if the pieces are large. Place in a saucepan with the sugar, orange juice and liqueur. Heat gently until the sugar has dissolved.

Blend the arrowroot with a little water and add to the pan. Bring to the boil, stirring, and cook until the sauce thickens. Stir in the butter.

NOT SUITABLE FOR FREEZING.

Orange Peel

Serve with ice cream and steamed puddings.

MAKES 300 ML/½ PT

300 ml/½ pt orange juice
1 tbsp arrowroot
2 tbsp chopped candied orange peel
1 tbsp orange liqueur (optional)

Blend a little of the orange juice with the arrowroot in a saucepan then add the remaining juice. Bring to the boil, stirring, and simmer until thickened and clear. Stir in the candied peel and the liqueur, if using.

SUITABLE FOR FREEZING.

Orange and Rum Butter

A basic orange butter. Orange liqueur or brandy could be substituted for the rum, if preferred. Serve with Christmas pudding, pancakes or steamed puddings.

MAKES ABOUT 225 G/8 OZ

125 g/4 oz unsalted butter
125 g/4 oz light soft brown sugar
1 finely grated rind of orange
Juice of ½ orange
2 tbsp rum
1 tbsp boiling water

Cream the butter and sugar together until light and fluffy. Add all the remaining ingredients and beat until well blended.

SUITABLE FOR FREEZING.

Cherry Liqueur

If a less sweet sauce is required, leave out the sugar or use commercial cherry compote. Serve over pancakes, ice cream or fruit fritters.

MAKES ABOUT 150 ML/¼ PT

175 g/6 oz black cherry jam
1 tbsp demerara sugar
1 miniature bottle of cherry brandy
1 tbsp lemon juice
1 tbsp cornflour
3 tbsp water

Place the jam, sugar, cherry brandy and lemon juice in a saucepan and heat gently to dissolve the sugar.

Blend the cornflour with the water and stir into the pan. Continue stirring until the mixture comes to the boil then reduce the heat and cook for about 3–4 minutes. Cool slightly before serving.

NOT SUITABLE FOR FREEZING.

CHAPTER THIRTEEN
What Goes with What

THIS COMPREHENSIVE LISTING is a guide to which sauces are good accompaniments to a variety of dishes. The foundation sauces in Chapter Three are not included here – see pages 16–22 for their applications.

BACON

Aurore 24
Barbecue 50
Blue Cheese 63
Cumberland 30
Gooseberry 54
Mustard 32
Pineapple and Green
Pepper 55
Spiced Ginger 55
Sweetcorn 39
Tangy Redcurrant Relish 59

BEEF

Barbecue 50
Basic Curry 26
Bercy 24
Black Bean 48
Bordelaise 27
Bourguignonne 28
Diable 32
Horseradish 60
Italienne 28
Lyonnaise 31
Madeira 33

Mustard 32
Peperoni 37
Périgueux 33
Poivrade 29
Quick Beef and
Mushroom 28
Ravigote 57
Red Wine and Paprika 40
Red Wine Marinade 65
Romaine 40
Satay 50
Spicy Marinade 65
Sweet and Hot Mustard 32
Teriyaki 48
Tomato and Marjoram 40

CHICKEN

Aïoli 57
Apricot Curry 54
Aurore 24
Barbecue 50
Basic Curry 26
Bercy 24
Boiled Salad Dressing 62
Bolognaise 44
Broccoli with Lemon 35
Caper 27
Charcutière 29
Chasseur (Huntsman's) 30
Chivry 24
Coconut and Chilli 49
Cold Creole 35
Curried Parsnip and
Celery 39

Diable 32
French Dressing
(Vinaigrette) 62
Korma 49
Leek and Bacon 43
Lemon Marinade 65
Mexican Green Salsa 47
Mushroom and Sherry 41
Peperoni 37
Ratatouille 37
Ravigote 57
Romaine 40
Satay 50
Spiced Ginger 55
Spicy Marinade 65
Supreme 29
Sweet and Hot Mustard 32
Sweet and Sour 48
Sweetcorn 39
Tarragon and Parsley 38
Teriyaki 48
Thousand Island 64
Tomato and Marjoram 40
Tomato and Mozzarella 41
Tomato Dressing 64
Tonnata 58
Vegetarian Pasta 45
Watercress and Walnut 63
White Wine Marinade 64

DUCK

Apple 52
Apple and Sloe 52

Bigarade 26
Cherry Brandy 52
Orange 53
Pineapple and Green
Pepper 55
Starfruit and Pineapple 55
Sweet and Sour 48
Tangy Redcurrant Relish ... 59

EGGS

Aurore 24
Basic Curry 26
Boiled Salad Dressing 62
Chivry 24
Cold Creole 35
Cold Curry 57
Curried Parsnip and
Celery 39
Minted Pea Purée 38
Mornay 31
Mushroom and Sherry 41
Onion Cream (Soubise) 30
Ratatouille 37
Spinach 35
Thousand Island 64
Tomato and Lentil 41
Tomato Dressing 64
Tonnata 58

FISH

Aïoli 57
Aurore 24
Avocado 62

Basic Curry	26
Beurre Blanc	26
Broccoli with Lemon	35
Caper	27
Celeriac and Coriander	36
Chivry	24
Cocktail	65
Crab	33
Cucumber and Dill	36
Curried Parsnip and Celery	39
French Dressing (Vinaigrette)	62
Gooseberry	54
Horseradish	60
Lemon Marinade	65
Mornay	31
Mushroom and Sherry	41
Quick Lemon and Caper	58
Ravigote	57
Red Peppercorn and Cream	38
Rémoulade	58
Rich Prawn Sauce with Dill	25
Romaine	40
Satay	50
Smoked Salmon	27
Sour Cream and Chive	60
Tarragon and Parsley	38
Tartare	58
Tomato Dressing	64
Vegetarian Pasta	45
Whipped Butter	33
White Wine Marinade	64

FRIED AND BATTERED FISH

Aïoli	57
Raita	57
Sweet and Sour	48
Tartare	58

FRUIT, PIES, PUDDINGS, ICE CREAM, PANCAKES AND MERINGUES

Blackberry	75
Butterscotch	72
Caramel	72
Chantilly Cream	67
Cherry Liqueur	76
Chestnut	67
Chocolate	74
Chocolate Custard	69
Confectioner's Custard	69
Cream and Honey	73
Creamy Syrup	68
Economical Chocolate	75
Fluffy Lemon	73
Hot Chocolate	70
Hot Fudge	72
Hot Ginger	74
Jam and Arrowroot	73
Melba	75
Mousseline	68
Orange and Rum Butter	76
Orange Liqueur	76
Orange Peel	76
Peach and Passion	73
Quick Custard	69
Quick Toffee	74
Raspberry Coulis	74
Rich Orange Cream	67
Rum and Raisin	68
Sherry	68
Sweet White	70
Zabaglione	70

GAME

Apple and Sloe	52
Bigarade	26
Bordelaise	27
Charcutière	29
Chasseur (Huntsman's)	30
Cherry Brandy	52
Cranberry	59
Diable	32
Game	25
Orange	53
Plum	54
Poivrade	29
Supreme	29
Tangy Redcurrant Relish	59

GAMMON AND HAM

Bigarade	26
Blue Cheese	63
Charcutière	29
Cumberland	30
Diable	32
Gooseberry	54
Minted Pea Purée	38
Mustard	32
Plum	54
Savoury Marmalade	53
Tangy Redcurrant Relish	59

GOOSE

Apple	52
Apple and Sloe	52
Bigarade	26
Plum	54
Starfruit and Pineapple	55

INGREDIENTS FOR FLANS ETC

Leek and Bacon	43
Rich Prawn Sauce with Dill	25
Seafood	43
Supreme	29
Tomato and Olive	45

LAMB

Apricot Curry	54
Barbecue	50
Basic Curry	26
Black Bean	48
Caper	27
Coconut and Chilli	49
Italienne	28
Korma	49
Lyonnaise	31
Mint	59
Onion Cream (Soubise)	30
Ratatouille	37
Red Wine and Paprika	40
Redcurrant and Cider	53
Romaine	40
Satay	50
Spicy Marinade	65
Tangy Redcurrant Relish	59
Tomato and Marjoram	40

OFFAL

Cumberland	30
Italienne	28
Madeira	33
Périgueux	33
Robert	31

OMELETTES

Creole	47
Rich Prawn Sauce with Dill	25

PASTA

Bacon, Blue Cheese and Celery	43
Blue Cheese	63
Bolognaise	44
Chicken Liver	44
Chilli Beef	44
Cocktail	65

Curried Parsnip and Celery 39
French Dressing 62
Leek and Bacon.................43
Mornay 31
Pesto 49
Quick Lemon and Caper 58
Ratatouille 37
Rémoulade 58
Seafood 43
Sour Cream 63
Spanish 45
Spinach 35
Thousand Island 64
Tomato and Marjoram 40
Tomato and Mozzarella......41
Tomato and Olive 45
Tonnata 58
Vegetarian Pasta 45
Watercress and Walnut 63

PORK
Apple 52
Apple and Sloe..................52
Apricot Curry 54
Barbecue 50
Basic Curry 26
Black Bean 48
Cranberry 59
Creole 47
Cumberland 30
Gooseberry 54
Leek and Pepper 37
Lyonnaise 31
Mustard 32
Orange 53
Pineapple and Green Pepper 55
Poivrade 29
Ratatouille 37
Red Wine 64
Red Wine and Paprika........40
Robert..............................31
Savoury Marmalade...........53
Spiced Ginger 55
Spicy Marinade.................65
Spinach............................35
Sweet and Hot Mustard 32
Teriyaki............................48
Thousand Island 64
Tomato and Marjoram 40
Tomato and Mozzarella......41

RICE
Bolognaise 44
Chicken Liver 44
Chilli Beef 44
Gado-Gado 50
Leek and Bacon.................43
Seafood 43
Spanish............................45
Thousand Island 64
Tomato and Lentil 41
Watercress and Walnut 63

SALADS
Aïoli 57
Avocado 62
Blue Cheese......................63
Boiled Salad Dressing 62
Cocktail............................65
Cold Curry 57
French Dressing (Vinaigrette) 62
Rémoulade 58
Sour Cream 63
Sour Cream and Chive.......60
Thousand Island 64
Waldorf 60
Watercress and Walnut 63

SAUSAGES
Barbecue 50
Creole 47
Mexican Green Salsa..........47
Sweet and Hot Mustard 32
Tomato and Marjoram 40

TURKEY
Basic Curry 26
Cold Curry 57
Cranberry 59
Cumberland 30
Lemon Marinade 65
Plum................................54
Redcurrant and Cider 53
Spicy Marinade.................65
Sweet and Sour.................48
Watercress and Walnut 63
White Wine Marinade 64

VEAL
Bercy...............................24
Bourguignonne 28
Chasseur (Huntsman's)......30
Tonnata............................58

VEGETABLES AND VEGETARIAN
Aïoli 57
Apricot Curry 54
Aurore 24
Avocado 62
Bacon, Blue Cheese and Celery 43
Bagna Cauda....................47
Barbecue 50
Basic Curry 26
Bercy...............................24
Beurre Blanc 26
Blue Cheese......................63
Boiled Salad Dressing 62
Broccoli with Lemon 35
Carrot 35
Celeriac and Coriander......36
Celery 39
Chivry 24
Coconut and Chilli.............49
Cold Creole 35
Creole 47
Cucumber and Dill.............36
Curried Parsnip and Celery 39
French Dressing (Vinaigrette) 62
Gado-Gado 50
Garlic and Parsley 36
Korma 49
Leek and Pepper 37
Minted Pea Purée..............38
Mornay 31
Mushroom and Sherry.......41
Mustard 32
Onion Cream (Soubise)......30
Peperoni 57
Raita 47
Ratatouille 37
Red Wine and Paprika........40
Romaine 40
Sour Cream 63
Sour Cream and Chive.......60
Spinach............................35
Sweetcorn 39
Tarragon and Parsley 38
Thousand Island 64
Tomato and Lentil 41
Tomato and Marjoram 40
Tomato and Mozzarella......41
Tomato and Olive 45
Tomato Dressing................64
Vegetarian Pasta 45
Waldorf 60
Watercress and Walnut 63
Whipped Butter 33

Alphabetical List of Sauces

A
Aïoli 57
Apple 52
Apple and Sloe 52
Apricot Curry 54
Aspic Jelly 12
Aurore 24
Avocado Dressing 62

B
Bacon, Blue Cheese and Celery 43
Bagna Cauda 47
Barbecue 50
Béchamel 17
Beef and Mushroom, Quick 28
Bercy 24
Béarnaise 22
Beurre Blanc 26
Bigarade 26
Black Bean 48
Blackberry 75
Blue Cheese Dressing 63
Boiled Salad Dressing 62
Bolognaise 44
Bordelaise 27
Bourguignonne 28
Bread 20
Broccoli with Lemon 35
Brown, Simple 17
Butterscotch 72

C
Caper 27
Caramel 72
Carrot 35
Celeriac and Coriander 36
Celery 39
Chantilly Cream 67
Charcutière 29
Chasseur (Huntsman's) 30
Chaudfroid 22
Cherry Brandy 52
Cherry Liqueur 76
Chestnut 67
Chicken Liver 44
Chilli Beef 44
Chivry 24
Chocolate 74
Chocolate, Economical 75
Chocolate, Hot 70
Cocktail 65
Coconut and Chilli 49
Crab 33
Cranberry 59
Cream and Honey 73
Creamy Syrup 68
Creole 47
Creole, Cold 35
Cucumber and Dill 36
Cumberland 30
Curried Parsnip and Celery 39
Curry, Basic 26
Curry, Cold 57
Custard, Chocolate 69
Custard, Confectioner's 69
Custard, Quick 69

D
Demi-glace 19
Diable 32

E
Egg Custard 21
Espagnole 19

F
French Dressing (Vinaigrette) 62
Fudge, Hot 72

G
Gado-Gado 50
Game 25
Garlic and Parsley 36
Ginger, Hot 74
Ginger, Spiced 55
Gooseberry 54
Gravy 19

H
Hollandaise 21
Horseradish 60

I
Italienne 28

J
Jam and Arrowroot 73

K
Korma 49

L
Leek and Bacon 43
Leek and Pepper 37
Lemon and Caper, Quick 58
Lemon, Fluffy 73
Lemon Marinade 65
Lyonnaise 31

M
Madeira 33
Marmalade, Savoury 53
Mayonnaise 22
Melba 75
Mexican Green Salsa 47
Mint 59
Mornay 31
Mousseline 68
Mushroom and Sherry 41
Mustard 32
Mustard, Sweet and Hot 32

O
Onion Cream (Soubise) 30
Orange 53
Orange Cream, Rich 67
Orange Liqueur 76
Orange Peel 76
Orange and Rum Butter 76

P
Pea Purée, Minted 38
Peach and Passion 73
Peperoni 37
Périgueux 33
Pesto 49
Pineapple and Green Pepper 55
Plum 54
Poivrade 29
Prawn with Dill, Rich 25

R
Raspberry Coulis 74
Raita 47
Ratatouille 37
Ravigote 57
Redcurrant and Cider 53
Redcurrant Relish, Tangy 59
Red Peppercorn and Cream 38
Red Wine Marinade 65
Red Wine and Paprika 40
Rémoulade 58
Robert 31
Rum and Raisin 68

S
Satay 50
Seafood 43
Sherry 68
Smoked Salmon 27
Sour Cream and Chive 60
Sour Cream Dressing 63
Spanish 45
Spicy Marinade 65
Spinach 35
Starfruit and Pineapple 55
Supreme 29
Sweet and Sour 48
Sweetcorn 39

T
Tarragon and Parsley 38
Tartare 58
Teriyaki 48
Thousand Island Dressing 64
Toffee, Quick 74
Tomato Dressing 64
Tomato, Fresh 20
Tomato and Lentil 41
Tomato and Marjoram 40
Tomato and Mozzarella 41
Tomato and Olive 45
Tonnata (Tuna Fish Mayonnaise) 58

V
Vegetarian Pasta 45
Velouté 20

W
Waldorf 60
Watercress and Walnut 63
Whipped Butter 33
White, Basic 17
White, Sweet 70
White Wine Marinade 64

Z
Zabaglione 70